GREAT
JOURNEYS
OF THE WORLD

GREAT JOURNEYS
OF THE WORLD

ERNIE DINGO

•

EVELYN GLENNIE

•

DAMIAN GORMAN

•

TONY ROBINSON

•

JULIET STEVENSON

•

SANDI TOKSVIG

Photographs by
TOM OWEN EDMUNDS

•

BBC BOOKS

Endpapers: Sand dunes of the Sahara near Merzouga in Morocco
Frontispiece: Pulguksa Temple, Kyongju, in South Korea

Maps by Line & Line

The photograph on page 43 is by Russell England

Quotations from the writings of Isabelle Eberhardt in Juliet Stevenson's
essay are taken from Isabelle Eberhardt, *The Oblivion Seekers*,
trans. by Paul Bowles (Peter Owen, 1988),
Annette Kobak, *Isabelle: The Life of Isabelle Eberhardt* (Penguin Books, 1988)
and *The Passionate Nomad: The Diary of Isabelle Eberhardt*,
trans. by Nina de Voogd (Virago, 1987).

Published by BBC Books,
a division of BBC Enterprises Limited
Woodlands, 80 Wood Lane, London W12 OTT

First published 1994

ISBN 0 563 37050 5

Set in Bembo by BBC Books
Printed and bound in Great Britain by Butler & Tanner Limited,
Frome and London
Colour separations by Radstock Repro Limited, Midsomer Norton
Jacket printed by Lawrence Allen Limited, Weston-super-Mare

CONTENTS

THE ZAMBEZI
Sandi Toksvig

Choosing the Zambezi river for a novice canoe trip is a fundamental mistake. The 'river of the gods' flows for 1700 miles through four countries (one of which is at war and another just recovering), skirts past a fifth, and throughout its length and breadth there are over nine hundred species of wild animal who might wish to interfere with you. I blame my father.

When I was about eight years old my family and I were living in suburban Americana, in Westchester county outside New York City. My father was foreign correspondent for Danish Television and had an office at the United Nations. One day he arrived home with a large wooden canoe strapped to the roof of the Pontiac.

'I have bought the canoe which charted the Zambezi,' he announced proudly.

I think it was a measure of my father that none of us questioned this. To this day not one of us knows where he bought it, for how much or why he believed it had done this great deed. The mahogany canoe came in two halves which locked together with two brass handles, three hooks and a rubber seal. Dad put the thing together and popped it in our paddling pool in the garden. There was just room for the 'bean pod', as it became known, to turn a full circle and I have a wonderful photograph of my beloved father that night, drinking whiskey in his canoe and looking as happy and relaxed as I ever saw him.

*Sandi punting across to the western shore of the Zambezi
at the crossing point at Libonda in Zambia.*

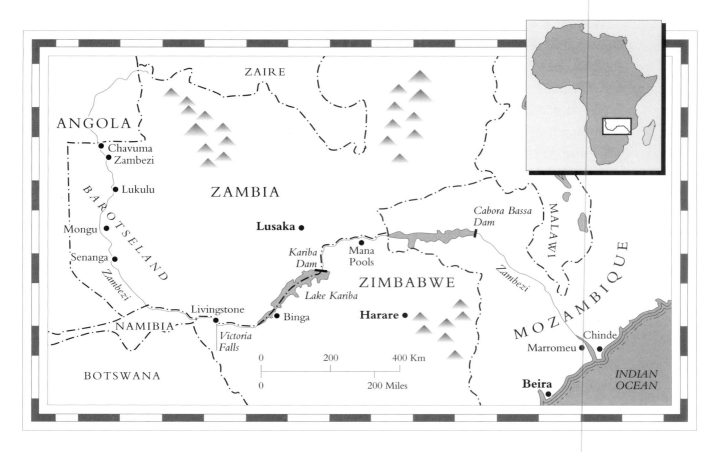

I don't remember the bean pod ever touching water again after that night. But for twenty-five years the wretched vessel followed us from country to country as we lived a life of perpetual motion. When my father died, the canoe was moved to my mother's new home. We placed the bean pod in the rafters of her garage and forgot about it.

Then I was asked if I wanted to make a 'great journey'. I suppose I could have contemplated more comfortable voyages – a cruise up the Nile, some splendid train journey with a lot of bouncy velour seating – but I thought of Dad's canoe. Mum and I got it down and dusted it off.

I had spent part of my childhood in Africa and still had distant memories of dirt tracks and dust spraying from Land Rover wheels, but things have changed for the Western traveller since the early 1960s. You would think that travel was now easier, but it is quite the reverse. In my mother and father's day there were establishments in London entirely devoted to the outfitting of travellers heading for tropical climes. They dispensed clothing, mosquito nets and advice which prepared the mind and body for discomfort and hardship ahead. But today, we in the pampered West have lost the ability to travel properly. Even on exotic holidays we expect a certain level of hygiene, food and accommodation. Without it we are fearful and ill prepared. I gathered together a plethora of water purifiers, dried blood and spare fishing line and began malarial hallucinations of disaster in the bush. I didn't set out for a great journey, I set out to survive.

You can never know what stuff you're made of until your back is against the wall. It is disturbing, however, to feel put to the test on the flight out. For those of you who haven't flown British Airways long distance, let me give you this piece of vital information – not all seats recline. As the steward informed me, 'In theory, they all recline', but row 38 does not. Row 37, however, reclines right into row 38. I spent twelve hours with my back against the wall, sitting bolt upright, my dinner under my chin and counting the hair follicles on a balding man with a skin condition in front. I was an unhappy woman. At Lusaka airport, I discovered that my treasured and restored canoe had been sent to Frankfurt by mistake and would be some days in joining me. It was not an auspicious start.

I was to spend one night at a game lodge outside Lusaka before taking a light aircraft up to the source of the river. We bumped along what is one day promised to be a road. The red dust track was a hive of activity. Twelve men in tan uniforms walked beside a bulldozer, holding a stick between them. I was told they hope to get the road finished before the rainy season. I didn't know when that was, but it seemed unlikely. A man walked past with a chartreuse armchair on his head as he joined crowds on the rubbish-strewn acres of barren land along the roadside. This was Africa, but not the postcard variety.

At Lilayi Lodge, the Africa of the movies raised its head. Impala, kudu and zebra wandered about while frogs did unspeakable things in the swimming pool. Lunch consisted of crocodile tail in cream sauce, and dinner was zebra curry. There was much discussion about the minimum equipment to be taken for the next day's flight. Tomorrow everything and everyone would be weighed before take-off. I skipped pudding as a zebra wandered past in search of a lost relative. That night, the thatched roof of my rondavel was alive with activity. Things scratched, buzzed and slithered whilst outside giant eland gnawed away at the eaves. I chanted the mantra of my liberal, Western rules of conservation until a large slimy thing entered my toilet bag and I killed it with my World Wildlife Fund membership card.

The flight to the remote North-western Province of Zambia, where the Zambezi begins, lasts a bumpy two and a half hours. I had been thrilled at the prospect of seeing the great plains of Africa from the air as herds of wildebeest stampeded below. I saw not one creature. Only mile after mile of scrubby, identical plain. Even the National Parks of Zambia have been systematically depleted by the modern poacher. There was a time when the land below teemed with every kind of wildlife; now, in one generation, it had gone. I resorted to a month-old copy of the local paper. My stars advised me to 'be more sensible'.

The interesting thing about the source of the Zambezi is that it's a bit of a movable feast. Everyone agrees that it lies on Kalene Hill in North-western Province, but exactly where is open to interpretation. When the wife of Zambia's President visited, she went to a spot at the bottom of the hill – mainly because it was less muddy. A battered metal sign with peeling paint heralded the dirt road up to the source. A group of men appeared from a small collection of hand-made huts which were covered in thatch with varying degrees of success. A bright copper-coloured stick in the ground with a small jar suspended from a string swung at the roadside: it was a subtle advertisement for the availability of local hooch. The official 'custodian of the source' had clearly taken some advantage of this. Wearing a green and yellow nylon tracksuit sporting the logo of the Wexford Hockey Association the gaunt man appeared, grinning. He only had one eye but it had moved somewhere to the back of his head; he was, in local parlance, 'well cooked'. The custodian solemnly handed me a disintegrating visitors' book to sign with a Biro which he had been chewing for some time. Children gathered, as they would everywhere I stopped in Africa, dressed in the ragbag of well-intentioned but misguided aid I was to see in every country. One small boy wore a pair of shorts which now consisted only of a drawstring and two pockets.

Three miles further down the road I came at last to my holy grail – the source of the Zambezi. There were no signs or arrows: the tourist was left to get on with the search alone. My host Peter Fisher, a local farmer, and I wandered down through riverine forest which became darker and darker. Across springy, moss-covered ground he followed a path which I found indistinguishable. We passed several muddy pools of water which were the Zambezi, but Peter ploughed on through the downtown Los Angeles of mosquitoes. The ground itself began to make bubbling noises as we climbed higher over ground made up of tree roots laced together with vegetation which hovers above the fledgling river.

The source itself was something of an anti-climax. A massive tree had plunged down on to the forest floor. Below its raised root, a pool of stagnant water lay in a small dark wooden cave. It was the beginning of a 1700-mile journey which was to leave me exhausted, dehydrated and frightened to death.

My canoe had now concluded its European tour and arrived. At a narrow strip of the river I launched the gleaming vessel. I paddled past washing women, waved happily and banged straight into a spike on the underside of the bridge – the planks had been driven into the supports with lethal wooden spikes which now attempted to entangle my flesh. I doubt anyone had ever planned for a canoe to come this way. I was ready for real fear. I was ready for Angola.

More specifically, the journey to Angola. North-western Province sits tucked up in a corner next to Angola and Zaire. The Zambezi inconsiderately departs from Zambia for a while and meanders off into the war-torn countryside of Angola. The border was due to close in an hour, but this did not deter Peter Fisher. Scraped through the bush, the dust roads in the province are a tyre manufacturer's dream: there must be a need for a thousand new purchases every mile. Pete likes to drive fast. I had realized you could get killed in Angola, but no one had mentioned it could happen on the way there. We hurtled to the border and with a bang took out a chicken foolish enough to step in our way. Pete skidded to a halt at the police station. I wanted to say he had done well but I knew a chicken with a different story.

The small immigration hut stood in the shadow of a straw watchtower built astride a 20-foot high termite mound. A Barclays Bank sign in the window announced 'Kwacha

Travellers Cheques accepted here'. (This would have been news to my local Barclays, who had denied all knowledge that the Zambian currency, the Kwacha, even existed.) The bespectacled officer in charge was of a nervous disposition. He was from military intelligence, although the intelligence part was not featuring heavily. He spoke to two young lads in camouflage uniforms lounging against the barrier.

'Quick! Get inside. I don't want them to see you in your camouflage.'

This seemed to mitigate against the purpose of camouflage, but he moved on to requests for official documents. I showed him my temporary Zambian press pass which appeared to have been printed with a 'Let's play post office' kit, a potato and a very old ink pad. As he studiously studied the pass, a two-year-old boy ducked in and out of the sentry box window and a man on a bicycle crossed over from Angola unchecked. The arbitrary national divisions mean nothing to the local Lunda people, who follow tribal lands and ignore our foolish addiction to paper. After a great deal of discussion I was permitted to proceed down to the border.

A concrete bridge over the Jimbe river connects Zambia to Angola. In the centre of the bridge, a faded green line marks the actual border. Sunning themselves on the Angolan parapet were two men – one in army fatigues and the other cutting a dash with jeans and a military beret. They both packed huge pistols and had a vaguely cooked look about the eyes. The beret was the local Angolan Commissioner of Police and the other the local commander of the Unita forces. These were the warmongers of Angola and they wanted to say hello. I stepped over the line into Angola to have a 'chat' with Unita.

'It is safe to follow the Zambezi here,' they both assured me.

'Come to Angola. It is peaceful,' said the Commissioner of Police, adjusting his gun. 'Ah!' he remembered, 'but there are no bridges. All the bridges are gone.'

It seemed a perfect excuse not to trespass any further, and I headed back to Zambia. As I turned for a last look at the crossing, I saw Unita waving cheerfully goodbye with one hand and clutching their pistols with the other. Extraordinary.

We went home and found a rat in the utility room. Peter's wife Lynn was taking blood from a guest for a malarial test while waiting for a radio message in this land of no communications. I browsed through a copy of *Your Medical Guide for Africa* and found a whole series of deeply unsavoury photographs of potentially lethal diseases and some far too detailed advice. I had just reached 'ice enemas' when the gong sounded. It was time for dinner.

From its humble beginnings the Zambezi gets a grip on itself pretty quickly. You haven't got to travel very far for the river to have powered into a series of small rapids. Bored with the slow bubble of its beginning, the water surged over smooth slabs of rock and down into a large pool before flowing on round the corner downstream. Here the river seemed like fun. The missionaries were out in force with kids from the local school gliding across the waters on large inner tubes. The Canadian teacher, wearing a loud whistle and a white pith helmet with a solar-powered fan built into the front, assured me there were no crocodiles 'at the moment'. The kids seemed to be having fun, so I said I was ready to take my first baptism in the river – and then realized this was a poor term to use with missionaries.

The current was far stronger than it appeared from the bank, and I found I could not swim clutching several pounds of inflated rubber. The water was a very dark brown, making it impossible to see what was below. My feet found jagged rocks and shot back up to the surface in a surfeit of imagined horrors. In the end I had to be rescued by Bruce, another Canadian missionary. Ah the indignity of my white, flabby body hauled from the river across the rocks to the shore.

It was my day for testing the new-found waters of my fearlessness. Disdainful of anything which might have pretensions to the status of a road, Peter headed the Land Rover across lava-like terrain to reach the first bridge across the Zambezi. Above a home-made fishing dam of spikes and poles was a wooden construction about two feet wide, made of a lashed assortment of poles and sharp things. At one time it had featured a hand rail in its design, but this had long since sagged wearily into the river. Each pole beneath my feet was of a unique size, and the entire collection rolled and shifted under my weight as I attempted to navigate to the other side. The insistent sun had cracked and splintered the dry wood, forcing me to alternate tightrope acting with rather more demeaning crawling. Below me a line of broken sticks with jagged edges poked up from the river. It was not a place to linger. A man loped past me carrying a bicycle. I was a clumsy, urban Westerner and the sound from the river was laughter.

I was to skim past Angola by light aircraft, flying with the Wings of the Morning Mission. From the air the river snaked beneath the trees amidst wide green areas of flood plain. It looked like the back nine at a Surrey golf course, only with fewer customers. Every fifteen minutes, pilot Steve called in his location on the radio to his long-suffering wife.

'If you go down out here, someone needs to know where to find you,' he said comfortingly.

He told me that his only severe problem in the air had been a cerebral malarial attack which had paralyzed him at 5000 feet (1524 metres). I looked down at the dense bush below and began to pay much more attention to the instrument panel.

We landed on the spongy sand strip which passed for a landing site at Lukolwe Mission. Steve had pointed it out in the distance. All I could see was trees until we actually hit the sand. I could see why you need faith for these missions.

The Zambezi had been for its unaccompanied Angolan detour and now returned to Zambia with a boom into the Chavuma Falls. It had gathered speed and size on the way and was by now wide and impassable except by pontoon. In the company of two elderly Irish mission sisters I headed across the waters with a Land Rover resting on oil drums strapped together by a large metal frame. Powered by a small outboard, we made slow progress. Then the engine gave up and we made no progress at all. We were stranded between nowhere and nowhere on the great river highway. Running low on water, we filtered some from the river in my army filtration kit. It tasted as though it had passed through several people already.

Eva and Emily are remarkable white-haired old ladies. They have been missionaries for over forty years along the banks of the Zambezi, yet they retain an Irish lilt to their voices and Sunday School best sense of dress. In her seventies, Eva is the 'maintenance officer' of the mission. She has built, plumbed and wired their home and drives the Land Rover with a ferocity which made Peter Fisher look timid. The injection tube for the diesel on the vehicle had broken as they arrived. Eva pulled out some drip feed tubing from the glove compartment and set about making repairs. As the Zambezi passed beneath my feet, she gave me some advice if I was ever taken by a croc.

'Offer him your arm, not your leg. Then you might still get away.' Having a limb policy with regard to crocodiles had never occurred to me.

In their high-necked white blouses and low-heeled sandals the sisters spun stories of emergency Caesareans and other medical matters as the pontoon swayed on the river. Perhaps it was the heat of the day, or not having eaten for nine hours, or being stranded on a pontoon with the blessed, but I began to feel I had an excess of information about the various incision points in female genitalia. Eva put on a home-made gospel tape from an Irish mission in Japan. The young black lad running the engine fussed over his charge.

'Ah!' said Emily, fondly looking at him. 'As we say – you're bad with them but you're worse without them.'

A guitar strummed for the Lord, the Land Rover revved and my mind swam with emergency operations as we finally arrived at Chavuma Mission. Nothing in Africa runs to time. I was three days late for lunch, but no one seemed the least perturbed. A bevy of female Canadian missionaries fussed around us as the only man present said grace.

'Thank you, Lord, for the day we've had.'

I descended into unseemly giggles.

That night we camped by the river. The men bathed in the waters, soaping themselves all over and running at the river full pelt in some strange male competition. I settled for a paddle in my canoe followed by a moist tissue. A latrine with a wall of grass matting had been dug a hundred yards from camp. Several bricks had been placed around the hole and a toilet seat rested on top. It didn't fool me. The boys raced out as crocodiles were spotted up-river. The moon played across the waters. All the better for the crocs to see by.

From Lukolwe airstrip we flew downriver to the settlement of Zambezi which in these parts passes as a town. The control tower had long since been abandoned and was now only occupied by youngsters hoping for a better view of the plane. I was seeking the bridge at Chinyingi, which had appeared like a thin line across the river from the air. Yet another development for yet another mission. Built by an Italian priest, Father Crispin, it is a bizarre achievement. Chinyingi Bridge is a 3-foot-wide suspension bridge spanning several hundred feet across the Zambezi, several hundred feet in the air. It was built entirely of scrap begged and borrowed from the mines in the copper belt. This was not information which gave me any comfort as I proceeded to cross. The bridge bounced and swayed as the river appeared to move before my eyes. Below me, on a wooden pontoon, I could see a monk making his way across the river.

This was Father Charlie, a 300-pound (136-kilo) brother from Newark, New Jersey with a black beard so long it might itself have attempted to span the waters. Father Charlie does not use the bridge since he went through it one night. It seems the good father was returning to the mission with a crate of beer on his head; the combined weight of holy man and alcohol proved too much and the planks gave way. Father Charlie plunged into the river but managed to throw the beer forward to safety. As I clung to a thin wire in the centre of the swaying, fragile structure children ran past me to the mission. A sign on the opposite bank warns that no motorcycles are permitted on the bridge. I was pleased that they were adopting such stringent safety regulations.

My canoe and I were becoming casual users of light aircraft as I moved on to Lukulu airstrip further downriver. I was less confident, however, when we hit severe turbulence and I heard the pilot radio to his wife that he was 'suffering from my old problem'. Nuns flapping over the runway to greet us did not help. Another mission in another deserted spot. These enrobed women were from the Leperasarium.

'We have it all here,' said an elderly Irish nun. 'Fathers, brothers, sisters.'

'Nice to have the whole family,' I mumbled.

I waved goodbye to my Wings of the Morning pilots and turned to face a fresh pummelling of my internal organs.

With new guides I was heading for a fishing trip on the great river. The Land Rover headed off across sandy flood plain following no discernible track whatsoever. As my kidneys swapped places with my liver, my white guide shouted over the engine that our camp was right by the waters.

'The local Lozi people used to live there, but too many were taken by crocodiles,' she screamed in a piercing Afrikaner accent. I felt this was a poor selling point for a new client.

Tiger Camp was a strange combination of camping, civilization and total isolation. Right on the edge of a steep bank down to the river, it consisted of standard camping tents erected under individual thatched roofs. At the back of the tent a straw enclosure had been built in which, bizarrely, a flush toilet, sink and home-made shower had been placed. I found I was able to shower, use the toilet and look out of the window to the hippos on the river all at the same time.

Here is a strange fact. More people are killed by hippos every year than are hit by London buses. A campfire for the evening had been dug into a shallow pit to keep it out of hippo eye line. Apparently hippos hate fire and, if they see one, will tramp out of the water

Sister Maurice from the Catholic mission at Lukulu,
where the nuns run a hospital for lepers.

Overleaf: The elderly Chieftainess Mboanjikana of Barotseland,
elephant-hair fly whisk at the ready and still regal in her Western
cotton dress and cloche hat. Despite the introduction of a more
modern political system in Zambia, out here in the countryside
local chiefs remain the ruling élite.

and put it out. As I digested this information we set out to catch some local tiger fish. In the thatched bar area a UHF radio whistled and squawked and no one answered. We were in a communication wilderness.

A storm was approaching as we set out. I was preoccupied with keeping my canoe afloat and away from hippo and didn't pay a lot of attention to my fishing companion. Father J.C. was another American blessed person and rather better at the fishing than me. He showed me a 2-foot tiger fish he'd caught the day before.

'Can I have a bit?' I asked, having been hopeless at catching so much as a cold.

'No, this is for me,' he replied.

Five loaves, two fishes, but one of them is mine.

There was no rest on my whistle-stop tour. The rainy season was approaching and soon many parts of the river would become inaccessible. A local Lozi man, improbably called Kennedy, was to guide me on. He rode on the back of the pick-up truck, sitting on my upturned canoe and banging on the roof to indicate the next direction. It did not feel like a very politically correct arrangement, but I could find no distinguishing signs of direction on the endless flood plain and took his banging entirely on trust for hour after endless hour. Kennedy exhibited the kindness and gentle air I found among all the local people I met along the river. The Europeans had shafted them for generations, and still they smiled.

We passed a number of straw villages along the way. Some belonged to cattle farmers, and herds of long-horned beasts either traipsed across the plains or looked dolefully out from the squashed confines of corrals of lashed sticks. The houses on the water's edge were temporary accommodation for fishermen. Most resembled nothing so much as hayricks with a hole burrowed in the middle; come the rain and they would all be washed away. Kamikaze dogs from the villages threw themselves at my car tyres as we zipped through in a Western frenzy. The anti-rabies injection I had received did not prevent the disease: it merely allowed me seventeen hours to get to a doctor. So far we hadn't been able to get lunch within seventeen hours.

'We've arrived!' gushed my exhausting Afrikaner leader as we stopped in the middle of nowhere but closer to the river than before. This was Libonda pontoon in Barotseland, where we would cross to the western side of the Zambezi. There were new driving challenges ahead. Across the river by pontoon, and then into the unknown. Even Kennedy looked a little unsure as we ploughed through sand and lurched about in a whole new manner. Hardly a word was spoken as we evacuated to push the vehicle out of hostile soil patches. We were seeking the palace of Chieftainess Mboanjikana.

From the distance the royal village looked much like any other we had passed – a collection of straw houses gathered in a tight circle on a small rise – but Kennedy was confident. As we pulled into the village flames leaped from under the passenger seat in the vehicle. Nothing surprised me now, and we calmly blew them out. Two wires had been so rubbed together that they had ignited. I knew exactly how they felt.

Above and opposite: Lozi villagers near Lukulu.
The boy above is playing a marimba.

The palace of Chieftainess Mboanjikana lay behind a large enclosure of rush matting with a wide wooden gate. A man dressed mainly in crimplene stood guard holding a long, thin stick. I entered past a giant daub and wattle house with thatched roof which would not have looked out of place in Stratford-on-Avon. It was the old king's palace and no longer in use. The roof had begun to cave in and the building had been left to decline back into the soil.

Behind it, a surprisingly Western bungalow had been built as the new palace. I entered a small, dark room furnished with an old settee and single armchair. Several elderly men sat on the linoleum floor, wearing home-made berets of faded red cotton. It looked like a reunion of ancient paratroopers whose regiment had suffered severe financial embarrassment. There was a strong, acrid odour which burnt the nose. The Chieftainess appeared, apparently wearing a tea cosy on her head. A small, rounded woman in her eighties, she had the continuous physical shakes of a Parkinson's sufferer. There, in a lino-floored room with a tea cosy hat, she exuded regal behaviour and graciousness.

It is polite to 'clap' a chief as a mark of respect, but I hadn't quite gathered whether this took place before or after the handshake. Not wishing to offend, I clapped before and after but in a somewhat British way – clapping quietly and below the belt rather as if it hadn't happened at all. Chairs were procured for the garden. Branches of bright red flame tree were cut down to decorate her 'throne' as she sat facing west and the land of the people of Barotse. She changed her cosy for a kind of grey velvet 1920s' cloche and paraded out to the seats, flicking an elephant-hair fly whisk. I presented her with a packet of English tea, which she accepted with an English 'thank you'. This broke the ice and the entire court laughed at their ruler speaking English. We smiled, and I was permitted to sit in her presence. This caused some confusion to her Nduna or chief courtier, and while I remained seated he switched from calling me 'madam' to 'sir'. Between displays from the royal drummers the Nduna told me of the Chieftainess's problems. The young had no respect, no one followed tradition any more and things ain't what they used to be.

The Nduna was much preoccupied with a recent meeting of all the chiefs of Zambia in Lusaka. The seventy or so traditional rulers from all over the country had successfully demanded that the government should fulfil its obligations to support the chiefs both financially and politically. At last the long overdue monies for the tribal rulers to pay for their courts were to be handed over. Even the most ambitious of Zambian politicians have to recognize that, for the rural people at least, the chiefs still rule. The Chieftainess was uninterested in the present one-party system of an independent Zambia or speculation about an independent Barotseland. She longed for the return of the British, when there was order and calm. Her packet of tea rested on her lap as she shook and swatted flies away. The logo on the front of the tea box depicted an Edwardian couple taking tea at a lace-covered table; it was a symbol of old colonialism and totally incongruous. After some moments, the aged ruler simply decided she'd had enough and departed. I clapped and bowed as low as I could.

My final stop in Zambia before following the river on down to Zimbabwe was the Senanga Safari Hotel, where I was housed in another round hut with open thatched roof playing host to the only sorts of wildlife I had seen in Africa. The drain in the shower was simply a small hole in the wall to the outside. Come one, come all and join me in my hours of sleeplessness. I lit a mosquito coil and nearly choked to death as I debated dying of chemical poisoning or opening the door to a thousand night creatures. A huge fan, suspended above my bed, spun through the chemical haze. I imagined I was in Vietnam during the war with a helicopter making an awkward turn above my head after a particularly virulent napalm attack.

The hotel bar had a magnificent view of the Zambezi which followed me now like a faithful old friend. The management, however, had interrupted this vista with the largest satellite dish I've ever seen. This provided three people on the terrace the opportunity to watch reruns of very old BBC programmes and lent a slightly surreal air to the place. As I watched *The Late Show,* the hotel's drink supplier turned up. A jeepload of Namibian soldiers roared in over the nearby border with crates of beer and Fanta. No one said a word.

The following morning I waved goodbye to my flammable vehicle and once more packed the canoe on to a light aircraft. The bean pod was charting the Zambezi via every form of transport known to modern man. The Mongu airstrip held a distant memory of tarmac but was generally more familiar with sandy potholes and extravagant outbursts of scrubby grass. My plane stood in front of the customary collection of abandoned buildings and curious onlookers. A man who seemed to be nominally in charge, chased after the large crowd of children with a long length of rubber hosing to clear the runway. Look out, Western liberals coming through.

Nothing seemed real any more as I arrived in the land of the tourist who sees Africa from air-conditioned safety. At the Elephant Hills Hotel the door man wore a goatskin 'native' outfit. It seemed insulting, but he smiled. Everyone smiled. From my room I could see across the bush to the winding Zambezi and the spray of the falls in the distance. Down on the golf driving range warthog were grazing between the 50- and 100-yard markers. Hit a decent iron shot and you could easily get one in the eye. A young black man appeared at my door.

'I'm Special,' he announced.

This, it transpired, was his name and not an analysis of how he saw his position in life. Special cleaned my room. He was anxious to please and called me 'madam' at every opportunity. Special had a brother called Needs More who worked on another floor. The hotel was full of whites enjoying and blacks being special. For the tourist, the liberation of the black majority seemed primarily to have been translated into an anxiety at the front desk to do everything in triplicate.

I was unprepared for the falls to be quite so spectacular. It was like reluctantly reading a book as a child which everyone said was a 'classic' and then finding it was really rather good.

Sandi dancing at a political rally in a village between Mongu and Senanga.

Opposite: A masked dancer at the rally, held in support of a local MP.

Overleaf: Victoria Falls, or, as the local people rather more imaginatively call it, Mosi oa Tunya - the smoke that thunders.

I stood on a shelf of flat rocks where the river plunged into the Devil's Cataract and felt I was standing in the heart of a rainbow as water poured over the rocks and spray refracted in the light. It seemed obscene that Livingstone should have named it Victoria Falls. It had a perfectly good local name – Mosi oa Tunya, the smoke that thunders.

Clearly my canoe was not going to touch this part of the river, but I wanted to see the power of the falls for myself as it fell away into the gorge. A former Royal Marine helicopter pilot with the social skills of a small viper was to oblige. He waved me out from under the spinning blades of the chopper. I noticed there were no doors on the machine as he bellowed at me 'NOT repeat NOT' to put on my seatbelt.

That was the moment I should have calmly told him to switch off the engine and explain in a civilized manner what was happening, but I was too busy trying to find anything to hang on to as he began to lift the helicopter away from the ground. My right hand gripped the side of the seat as my left jammed on to the door frame. My left foot was half in and half out of the lip of the door as I sought something to push against. Before I could get my breath we were low over the trees and plunging down into the narrow gorge of the rapids. Steep rocks rose up on either side as we approached the fast-flowing water at a fantastic rate. In over the heads of several rafts full of helmeted holidaymakers and then round the corner to a bend in the river. The ground was composed of a jumble of sharp, irregular boulders. There was nowhere obvious to land.

'Get on the skid, NOW!' he screamed.

Without warning Mad Max spun the helicopter round some 20 feet in the air before lowering again. I grabbed my hat in my teeth and did as I was told. Clinging to the outside of the chopper I could not see the ground below me at all, yet I wasn't sure I didn't feel safer outside than in with this lunatic.

'GET OFF, GET OFF!' he shrieked, and I did. I stepped off into thin air and let go as the helicopter banked and swerved away. My right foot found a jagged rock and I crumpled down on to the ground. A raft with about ten people on it shot past in the rapids and immediately overturned. I was transfixed trying to count heads in the water. The raft was two or three hundred yards down river before I thought I could account for everyone. I didn't want to die and I didn't want to watch anyone else do it either. The Zambezi had turned into a monster and my only out was back in the helicopter. The steep gorge was unclimbable, and you couldn't exactly hitch a ride on the passing boats. From a puddle under a tree stump the river had built up enough fury to let nothing stand in the way. From above it looked majestic. Down in the gorge it was terrifying.

The crazed pilot returned, flying so low that I had to duck behind a rock to avoid the rush of wind. I clung petrified to the surface of a large boulder and wondered about trusting those in charge. The chopper swung around so that the open rear door was nearest to me. I gave myself no time to think. I realized if I didn't do it now I would never get back in again. I stepped on to the skid, trembling in every part of my being, and heaved myself in as the pilot once more swooped up away from the gorge.

It was boys' stuff. Boys' games to frighten girls, and it worked. I shook with sobs. Not just for the fear, but because this deranged man had destroyed the beauty of the place for me. It was a lesson in machismo and a male reaction to Africa which I was to find again and again. There is still great natural power along the Zambezi; but where I stood in wonder, many of the European men reacted by trying to beat it into submission.

Change of planes to the oldest to date. The ancient, threadbare seats had a lever marked 'recline'. It seemed only fitting that mine didn't function. We descended through dense cloud cover to temperatures of 114°F (46°C) and Lake Kariba. The lake is a massive sight from the sky and looks vaguely out of place in the area. Perhaps that is because it isn't natural. It was created in 1958 when the Kariba Dam was completed and the Zambezi permitted to flood across acres of pasture land. Eighteen thousand Tonga people were moved to higher ground as their villages were submerged by the flooding. Now these former fishing folk live on the edge of a vast body of water beside a hydroelectricity dam which provides them with neither water nor electricity.

At Binga airstrip, on the edge of the lake, I was collected by Alec, a local representative of the Save the Children Fund. He drove through some of the loveliest countryside I had seen so far. The hills in the distance broke up the monotony of the bush and the almost sealike waters of Lake Kariba were a tranquil sight. One of the SCF workers went off to collect his wife who had been bitten by a scorpion. I hadn't thought about scorpions till then. The temperature had now risen to 116°F (48°C). It was the perfect time to begin inspecting latrines.

If anyone ever asks me if it is worth giving money to charity I shall point them in the direction of a Blair latrine. These simple structures have revolutionized life in the villages and all at the cost of £13. A small, square building surrounds the usual hole in the ground. On the outside a single piece of pipe runs from the roof down into the hole. The flies are attracted into the hole (for obvious reasons) and then the natural current of gas forces them to exit via the pipe. Up they go and there is a piece of gauze covering the exit. Result – no escape, dead fly drops back into hole. There can be huge villages sharing one latrine and not a single fly in sight. It was a wonderful example of a little bit of aid going a very long way.

We stopped at a well for a brief respite. A woman drawing water into an old food container spoke English. She was a schoolteacher who had walked half a mile to get water for her students. Down the road the local water diviner, wearing a 'Wrestlemania' baseball cap, used two pieces of copper wire to seek out another well site. He told me the method had come to him in a dream; it is so hot that everyone dreams of water. We tried the 'Binga Supermarket' for refreshments but they didn't 'have any food at the moment'. We had come to the Siberia of these parts.

That evening, local whites invited me to dinner on their houseboat. The host spent his time complaining that when it was whites against blacks it was called racism and when it was

Lozi boy drumming in western Zambia.

Opposite: Tongan funeral procession at Binga. In the 1950s, thousands of Tonga people had to be moved to higher ground when the Kariba Dam was built and the Zambezi was allowed to flood their land. The former Tonga villages now lie under Lake Kariba.

blacks against whites it was called nationalism. Upstairs the whites sat stroking their beer bellies while downstairs two thin black men made the dinner. I wondered what we called that. Nothing had changed since my childhood. For generations the whites have held sway with their firepower, their superior resources and their seeming power to attain an afterlife. The blacks, in a small way, held their own with their knowledge of the land and its creatures and the fear the whites had of it. This relationship did not seem to have changed much. The blacks are still the guides through the hostile terrain and the whites are still preaching that theirs is the only way to salvation. I felt mutual distrust and mutual fear. Alcohol poured in a steady stream all night. For both black and white it was a vital crutch against the everyday struggle with life and themselves.

The next morning there was a strange atmosphere on board. A very hungover woman whom I hadn't seen before sat in a corner chain smoking. One of the men appeared to be slicing into the vessel with a chainsaw, while on the rocky shore a small truck with a large barrel and a petrol pump was being hand cranked by a half-naked black youth. Even at six in the morning he was sweating profusely. A small androgynous child wandered back and forth on board with a slightly vacant air. It was all rather creepy. I decided if they started chanting I was leaving.

It was with great relief that I departed to take my intrepid canoe out to the centre of the vast lake. It is an eerie place. The tops of small clumps of trees still break above the water surface to show where the villages of the Tonga people once stood. I tied my boat to a drowned treetop and watched the sun go down on the choppy waters. The grey wood of the trees seemed almost white in the dusk. The poet might well have seen an image of the hands of the Tonga people clawing up above the waters from the land where they once made their lives. At the Kariba Dam there is a plaque commemorating Operation Noah in which thousands of animals were moved away from the flood waters. There is nothing for the Tonga people.

Another pilot, another plane – this one a truly old lady which shed part of its instrument panel as we touched down at Mana Pools. At last I was heading for the postcard Africa – the wildlife reserve. From the air, the over-riding impression of Africa is brown. Even the river looks brown. You can almost feel the dust several thousand feet in the air. Trees stand aloof from one another in a more muted variation of the same earth colours. Every now and then there was a strip of brighter colour where a line of trees followed some unseen stream of water below the surface. I saw one lone elephant. He looked rather a forlorn chap leaning against a tree. The airstrip leapt out of the bush entirely unseen by me. I felt as if we had been sucked down rather than made any conscious decision about it.

My guide, Antony, had been provided by Hollywood central casting. Bleached blond shaggy hair, tanned muscular arms and legs which bulged from his minute shorts and T-shirt. From the back of an old pick-up I at last began to see some game. Skittish impala, packs of baboons, zebra, a family of elephants. On the banks of the Zambezi river,

Ruckomechi Camp may have had the luxury of a flush toilet,
but just to prevent anyone getting complacent the mosquitoes were
enormous: under the net was the only safe place.

Ruckomechi Camp was civilized camping. Small two-bedded rooms with steeply pitched thatched roofs and an almost half-timbered look to the cream outside. The large windows were covered in a large open mesh with two-inch holes in it. The mosquitoes in the area had to be enormous. Inside the room, behind a low wall, was an ancient shower, a flush toilet and a frog.

The frog was one of a series of frogs who preferred to live with me than without. He sat on the sink watching me do my business. A fellow frog had made himself at home on the indemnity form I was supposed to sign against the possibility of being maimed or somehow not departing the camp in the precise physical state I arrived in. I thought it was a paper-weight until it began croaking. The management also very kindly provided a checklist of more than nine hundred wild animals in the area which might want to mark your dance card.

Back on the river. The waters here were smooth with a gloss on them which made it quite difficult to discern what lay ahead. The hippos grunted and huffed all around the boat as crocodiles glided past. We came across a small herd of elephants washing by the Zambian side of the river. My dependable canoe took me and Adonis Antony within 15 feet of the gracious creatures. The largest bull flapped his ears and within a canoe length two young bulls began clashing tusks in mock battle. Further down and another herd of young bulls were taking the waters. About a dozen young bachelors tramped in the shallow waters, munching the long grasses. Emboldened by our previous success, we slipped the canoe in amongst the reeds and stepped out into the water in bare feet. I couldn't quite believe it was happening. This was not some Disney display or zoo. These were wild young males and we were sitting chatting a few feet away from them. The crocodiles had their chance but foolishly failed to spot me.

A giant bull elephant waded past en route from Zambia to Zimbabwe. Antony reassured me that nine out of ten animal attacks occur because the human has cut off the creature's route to escape or deep water. I decided not to ask about the remaining one out of ten. I had become marginally more confident and scanned the water carefully for any signs of disturbance. The hippos were most amenable and spent most of their time calling out their positions. I think we had a mutual desire not to share a canoe, and they kept their distance as irregular floating islands on the river. That night I slept in a bed under a tightly pulled mosquito net: so many forms of flying insect had landed on me during the day I'd felt I was doing an impersonation of the *Ark Royal*.

The following morning the rains had come and the camp manager was awash with doom and gloom. The roads would become impassable, supplies wouldn't get through and no doubt we'd all be eating each other within a week. I should have known then not to trust those who are apparently in charge. That is the trouble with Africa. Convinced that she will die if left to her own devices, the novice traveller wholeheartedly throws herself at the mercy of those with local knowledge and experience. Nowhere else would an intelligent person give up all responsibility and blindly follow the leader.

A small herd of elephants continues its ablutions on the Zambian bank of the Zambezi as Sandi and her guide paddle past.

Overleaf: A tusker in the Mana Pools National Park.

By lunchtime the rain had stopped. If it was the rainy season, then it was short. A young white guide called Colin, who appeared to be about twelve, was put in charge of a speedboat to take us to see a poached elephant. This time it was not a cooking method but a scene of horror. On a small deserted island midstream an executed elephant lay collapsed. It looked as if someone had let the air out of it. Both pairs of legs were crossed almost daintily but the skin of its giant body sagged and draped over the bones as if the stuffing had been removed. The indignity of bird droppings on its folds of skin surprised tears into my eyes, but it was the face which tried to bring my lunch back up. It had been simply cut clean away. The trunk lay separated from the head as if it had never belonged. A labyrinth of small bones in the skull had been planed right through with an axe. Flies buzzed incessantly and the rancid smell burnt my nose and mouth. It seemed wrong to be there. I thought humans weren't supposed to find elephant graves. As I turned my back, the flap of vultures' wings beat the smell of death into the air.

We moved upriver in search of more river inmates. Herds of hippos abounded, huffing and grunting in a loop tape of Tuba for Beginners. The sun was setting into one of those orange skies you see in movies about Africa but always think must have been done with filters. Momentarily I let slip my over-active imagination. It was beautiful. The river, the hippo, the sunset. It was at that precise moment that the outboard engine coughed and died.

Colin was calm. 'I think we're out of fuel.' This was clearly nonsense. One could not be out of fuel at dusk, miles from camp and on a stretch of water where scores of wild things are waiting to be formally introduced. Colin thought we might have enough left to 'get to the corner'. This was also absurd. Rivers do not have corners. The boat drifted downstream, out of control and into the stretch known locally as 'stump alley'. Now we had not only wildlife to contend with but a forest of submerged stumps which might wish to do battle with the hull. We had half an hour of light left. As Colin assured me that the camp would send help as soon as the sun set, we hit a submerged tree trunk with a thundering crash. With the single paddle on board we attempted to control the boat, but the Zambezi had a mind of its own.

Half an hour after dark no one had come and we were stuck on a sandbank. Colin, who was the only one who vaguely knew where we were, leapt out of the boat to push us off. It was odd to realize that on a par with the fear that one might get eaten by a crocodile is the horror that one might see it happen to someone else. I banged the side of the boat to keep hippos away and wondered if I should learn how to use the gun. Colin assured me he had at least five bullets. I wondered if crocodiles could count.

An hour and a half after sunset it was now so dark that nothing could be distinguished beyond the bows of the boat. The river, the banks and the sky had become one and we could predict nothing ahead of us. I have never seen such perfect darkness. It was a stage manager's dream. Colin decided he would fire into the air to try and attract attention. He advised me to sit with my fingers in my ears and my mouth open to protect against the loud

35

Sunset over the Zambezi is uncannily like a Hollywood movie director's concept of what an African sunset should look like.

Previous pages: Sandi in her canoe at dusk on the Zambezi, with the Zambian hills in the background.

report. I did, but couldn't help wondering if this was some final absurd indignity he was subjecting me to at will. The rifle butt knocked the slight young man back as he fired and then … nothing. No light, no sound, nothing. This was the moment when Colin recalled that the poaching patrols were out that night. They have a strict 'shoot first, ask questions later' policy and he decided he shouldn't have fired. We were now in more danger from humans than wild creatures. I began flashing SOS with an electronic camera flash. I found my mind was preoccupied with wondering if it was dot-dot-dot or dash-dash-dash first. Perhaps I was signalling OSO constantly, but then what did it matter? No one was coming to help anyway.

Two and a half hours after dark, a rescue boat finally appeared. The night was so impenetrable that we only spied it when the boat was almost upon us and it was at the moment we spied it that it too broke down. Our rescuers now needed rescuing themselves. We drifted away from one another as the lights from the camp came into view. A new danger emerged – the force of the river might sweep us past the camp, beyond which there was nothing for miles. We began to paddle with all our might. Out of nowhere a boat sped straight at us. It had no light and was coming at such speed that a collision seemed inevitable. We stood and screamed, and at the very last moment it swerved across our bow so that I might have reached out and touched the driver.

We paddled to the dock in a state of utter exhaustion. Back at camp, the manager had been to collect supplies in the jeep. Fifteen miles into the bush he had run out of fuel. These were the experts. We sat down to a steak dinner. It would have been flambé but I suspect they had run out of fuel.

That night my shoulders ached as if I had swum back dragging the boat behind me. No one slept well. A hundred yards from the camp a pride of lions were on the hunt. Their low roars began some distance away and then gradually moved closer as baboons led the escape, shrieking with fear. This was the sound of Africa I had expected and then was unprepared for.

Shaky with tiredness, I was heading for the final country in my journey, Mozambique. At Kariba international airport, the small Islander plane was parked next to a pile of elephant dung. It was not how I like my airports. Utterly unprepared, I was about to fly to a country with no electricity, no running water and far too many unexploded land mines to make travel a happy business.

We flew low all the way, winding between mottled brown mountains like the folds of a rather mangy fur coat. While the pilot appeared to be navigating with a road map the turbulence took its hold, shooting me out of my seat with such force that it undid my seatbelt. The landscape changed as we flew. At first the Zambezi meandered the way I had grown accustomed to, although there were far more dried out tributaries than before. They spread out along the banks as though giant trees had fallen there and left their impression in the brown earth. Then the lake created by the Cabora Bassa Dam gave an almost ocean-like presence in the middle of the river. By then rain had set in and the pilot kept asking me to 'look out for mountains'. Soon subtler swirls of deepening shades of brown and green spread out below. In place of scattered rondavels and small villages we began to see tin roofs on small low buildings. The fields were quilted affairs with low mud divides and furrow upon furrow of bright green sweet potato leaves. From the air it was hard to imagine the incessant civil war which until recently had raged in Mozambique.

Beira airport actually looked like an airport, albeit one just recovering from a long war. With peace only six months old, the UN presence was clear. Giant helicopters stood on the tarmac in the shadow of the rusting remains of a Russian military radar system. Wrecked Mig fighters littered the surrounding area. All signs were in the Portuguese of the former colonial power and the city had a faded feel about it. There was a shop-worn elegance to the city streets as we drove past once grand homes clasped tight with burglar bars on every window. Beira – former holiday capital and seaside resort.

Once more in the company of missionaries, I was to stay in their home. Every window and door in the place was barred and a young man in army fatigues stood guard in the garden with an AK47 rifle. It was, they told me, 'quite safe'. On a city street strewn with litter and abandoned children we dined in a restaurant with linen napkins and table cloths. The Picque Nicque restaurant with its neon sign of welcome and bottles of Mateus Rosé was hailed by our hosts as a sign of recovery. You had to take their word.

More flying. My new guide was at last a black person and a woman. Wadzanai Garwe (known as Wadzi) was a Zimbabwean doing development work in Mozambique, and one of the most delightful and articulate people I had ever met. At Marromeu airstrip we landed over the snapped remains of a Russian aid plane. The only vehicle available to take us around the town was a pick-up and Wadzi and I climbed into the back. Standing, holding on to the roof of the cab, I made the mistake of looking at her when we spoke and got smacked in the mouth by a tree branch. Wadzi was unperturbed. She said that the first thing aid workers learn is to accept discomfort.

Yet here in Marromeu there were things to take heart at. Less than one month after the main road had been cleared of land mines and reopened the local people had begun a street market. Wadzi and I wandered amongst all manner of goods for sale, laid out on rush mats or small stalls lashed together with strings. This was a fledgling economy beginning to spread its wings and take responsibility for itself. Small dried fishes were laid out next to sacks of mealie-meal, there were spring onions, sweet potatoes, jalapenos and garlic. Wadzi held up a beaded evening gown from a pile of aid clothing.

'Who can wear this?' she asked. 'What is the West thinking?'

Three men were carefully stripping rubber from an old truck tyre and using it to repair the soles of shoes, while others plaited home-made tobacco into neat coils of nautical-looking rope. For 2000 Metacash (about 20 US cents) I bought a shopping bag made from a US food aid sack. I wanted the stall holder to keep the change but Wadzi looked at me.

'Now Sandi, don't come playing the white man and ruin the economy in one day.'

She was right. It was something the locals felt the UN were already doing. The arrival of all the troops had already quadrupled the price of chickens and put them beyond the reach of ordinary families. Now there was a new problem. Many of the soldiers were offering local women the price of a chicken to sleep with them. AIDS was being spread not by the indigenous population but the saviours in the blue berets. There were stories of a thirteen-year-old girl who had been gang raped by twenty UN soldiers the week before. I realized I knew nothing. I had visited the great UN as a child with my father: it was supposed to be the great hope and salvation for the world. But the true answer for this ravaged country lay in the market and the optimism of the people. As I finished a soft drink I chucked the container in the air and crowds of children fought to grab it. Where water is important, then any container has a value. In Africa that is recycling.

At the Senna sugar factory we came upon the *Marie Celeste* of Marromeu. Lines of engines and carriages stood abandoned on the railway tracks. Huge pieces of machinery stood rusting in the yard as giant sections of tin roof crashed to the ground in the abandoned factory. With pure and simple malice the departing Portuguese had sabotaged the building so that it could not function.

Despite this catalogue of horrors, Wadzi was optimistic. She said the people had hope and determination and that they would survive. The wonderful thing is I believe she may be right – but it may well be despite the efforts of the outside world.

I set off to wave goodbye to the Zambezi. At the Chinde delta the 1700 miles of river finally exhausts itself into the Indian Ocean. We flew along the coast where the flood plain is deserted and Mozambique stands out as one long beach. Chinde is another colonial town well past its sell-by date. A few plate glass windows suggested a time when there had been shops. A derelict pump on a street corner stood under a broken neon sign announcing gasoline. The paint peeled on the wide verandas where once the sugar factory bosses sat sipping their pink gins and calling out orders to the servants. The new tenants seemed to have no particular occupation. A man idly swung a dead chicken between his legs, while another sat wearing red ski salopettes. It was 104°F (40°C). I went to look for the harbour master.

Resplendent in his white uniform, he stood on the steps of his official building waiting to welcome me. I needed a permit to put the bean pod through her final river paces. A clerk asked what tonnage I was. About 9½ stone (60 kilos) I replied. They didn't have the authority to write this, and so I was officially registered as one ton.

The harbour was a steamship graveyard. Rusting hulks lay beached all along the waterline and jagged pieces of metal sprouted from the sea. There had been some poor displays of navigation here. A large steel paddle steamer stood on giant blocks awaiting repairs. It had once ferried people for the Senna sugar company. A local aid worker was full of plans to refit the vessel and use it for tourists. I swatted away the continuous onslaught of flies and wondered at this fantastical plan. I had had my fill of European men with good intentions, sad hair and a perhaps unintentionally despotic attitude to the people they had come to help.

The actual 'harbour' was a small gap in the shoreline where it was possible to launch my canoe. The harbour master had called for a 'safety launch' to protect me. A large and almost totally unmanoeuvrable steam tramp chugged into view. It was covered in rust and every window in the wheel-house had been smashed. I hoped they would never have cause to rescue me. The tide was coming in fast, crashing against the ship skeletons. Across the water I could see the end of the Zambezi shoreline and the empty beginnings of the Indian Ocean. A huge crowd had gathered and the smell and flies were relentless. The harbour master stood in his pristine whites on the listing hulk of something ex-marine. It was entirely bizarre. I longed for great gulps of Nordic air, but I had come this far and was determined to paddle the last stretch of the impossible river.

At the edge of the Indian Ocean I set my canoe on the beach and plunged into the water. I was surprised to find it salty as the waves swept over me and tugged at my feet. I seemed to have lost the power of speech. My mind could not encompass the journey I had made from a trickle under a tree trunk to this crashing salt. I kept thinking about an elderly white missionary I had met on my journey. She had been in Africa for forty-two years, yet her vowels sounded fresh from the valleys of Kent. One day, a helicopter had arrived at the hospital in the bush to deliver a sick man. The glass machine hovered in the air as the man was lowered. The setting sun glistened on the windscreen. The children from the mission had never seen anything like it. They had no word for 'helicopter', so they called it 'child of aeroplane' and ran to tell the mission sister that the Lord Jesus had returned just as she had promised. She laughed at her own story, but I felt uncomfortable.

Kenneth Kaunda, former President of Zambia, once said that when the missionaries came to Africa, the Africans had the land and the missionaries had the Bible. The missionaries gave the Africans the Bible and told them to close their eyes and pray. When they opened their eyes again, the Africans found they had the Bible and the missionaries had the land. As I stood in the ocean at the end of my journey I thought of a biblical quote: 'All the rivers run into the sea; yet the sea is not full' (Ecclesiastes 1:7). The trouble is I don't think it means anything.

When it reaches the sea after its 1700-mile journey the Zambezi
flows into the warm, salty waters of the Indian Ocean.

THE KIMBERLEY
Ernie Dingo

God's own country, the Kimberley. 'On the seventh day God created the Kimberley,' according to some of my city mates who have travelled here, but they've got to be joking. I reckon he created this magnificent country the very first day he was in business! And I'm not the only one. The Aboriginal people of the Kimberley say this is Wandjina country, home of the Creator, and they know with absolute certainty that this is no ordinary piece of land. You only have to see it once to know they are right. There is definitely something out of the ordinary going on out there. Pretty land this ain't. And pretty history it hasn't had. But powerful, evocative and breathtaking is what it is.

I want you to know up front I am not from the Kimberley. Tribally I am a Wadjadi Yamatji, and my country, or what you mob would call my area, is down the road a bit, 1250 miles away, in the midwest region of Western Australia. I love my own country, and will always belong to it, but somehow that Kimberley red dirt is now in my blood and I've got to keep topping it up. The ancient land calls and, though I've been there several times, it still has a strong pull for me. It seems there is no choice given – it feels as if she has taken me as one of her own, and is trying to teach me something. That may sound strange to anybody from a Western culture, but this is strange country, believe me. Nothing is as straightforward as it seems. A journey here is more than merely parking yourself in front of scene after

Driving north in the western Kimberley 'up the corrugation known as the Gibb River Road'.

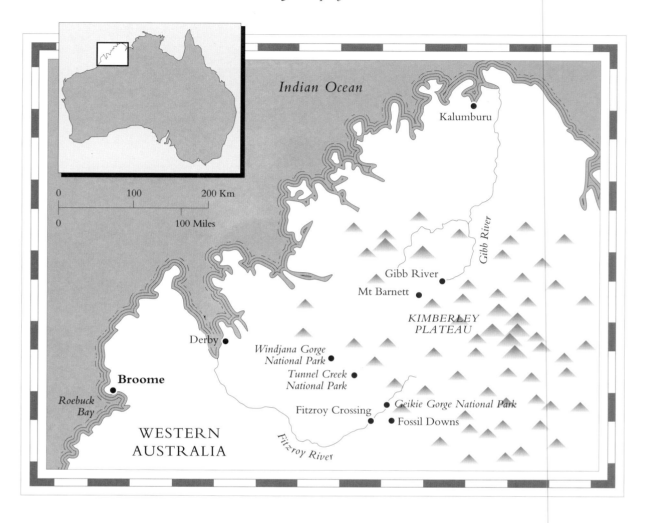

beautiful scene. A journey through the Kimberley is a journey to the soul of the Earth. The land is living. And to my way of thinking, you can count yourself privileged if she honours you with permission to enter.

So when I was offered the chance to return and stamp my feet on that special soil again, making a travel documentary, I suspected my lessons were not over. The land was calling and I was willing. My swag was rolled and my boots were packed before you could say, 'The Poms are coming.'

My journey for the documentary was to take me right across the remote and sparsely populated northwest corner of Australia, through red dirt country. When I say red, I mean red. There's no mistaking it. Pindan, the blood-red soil, has a quality all of its own. Beautiful. Rich. And with an astounding ability to stick to your clothes. Forget the whiter-than-white 'boss' look out here. If you don't take my advice, then just throw your clothes in the airport bin as you leave. Everything is bred tough in the Kimberley, dirt and all.

For my journey, the producer and his assistant were both British. Now you can't get anyone more Australian than me – I'm one of the originals – and to all Aussies a Pom is a Pom. Tough has never been a description we have applied to our British brothers and sisters. Quite simply, we regard it as our home-grown duty to find them all a little strange. I presume this developed when the first lot of Australians born after colonization started noticing a few differences between themselves and their British parents. Now it has become a national sport we all understand and enjoy. Without too much effort, I found myself wondering how it would be out in the scrub with them. We Aussies call a spade a spade, and proudly boast of our practical bent. Poms, we believe, will call a spade a shovel if they really *must* talk about such menial things, and then only if it has a napkin on and minds its manners! I also wondered how the porcelain-white producer's assistant intended to cope in the tropics. Should be interesting, I thought. Up here, the sun does a great job curling your sandshoes. There's even a lizard who finds the heat too much. He has developed a run where he stops every couple of steps, takes a front foot off the searing ground and waves it in the air as if to shake it cool. To us he is a Ta-Ta lizard, because he looks like a child leaving Grandma's. Quite plainly we're in scorched earth territory, the real kind, and the climate has never been kind to lily-white flesh. I hoped she was equipped with a very large hat, and a healthy respect for the sun.

I met up with the producer, his assistant and my Australian crew in Broome on the Indian Ocean. This was our starting place. And what a perfect place for beginnings – home of and inspiration for the history-making Aboriginal musical *Bran Nue Dae* (the title simply being the untutored Aboriginal way of spelling Brand New Day). It was a raucous, funny, irreverent and loud celebration of life, blackfella-style. My style. A style most Australians had never seen before. On the first Australian tour in 1990 I played the lead role of a cheeky old bugger, Uncle Tadpole, who was on a journey back to Broome, his beloved home town. As a result it has a special place in my heart.

One of *Bran Nue Dae's* songs describes the lifestyle here, and the sentiments are my sentiments to a T.

> Feel like going back home...
> Right now while the mangoes are ripe,
> Frangipanis are starting to bloom,
> And the Bluebone starting to bite.
>
> Hey mum I can just taste your fish soup and rice,
> I'm coming back home to you,
> Can't hack the pace of the city lights,
> Soon I'll be dreaming in Broome.

Who wouldn't want to be in such a paradise? Unlimited sunshine; fishing in Roebuck Bay; full moon at night across the bay creating a golden celestial stairway. Beautiful. And throw in a history which is the stuff adventure movies are made of: race riots; pearling masters dressed in white, living the fantasy life of colonial lords; cyclones destroying entire pearling fleets; pearl-diving triumphs; pearl-diving disgraces, with heavily pregnant Aboriginal women forced to choose between risking death in the deep or disobeying and then

Ernie standing by a statue of the founding father of Broome.

Pearl fishing was once the main source of employment in Broome, and many of the divers were Japanese. Every August the town still celebrates Shinju Matsuri, the Festival of the Pearl. Children enjoy dressing up for the grand parade, while the more muscular members of the community take part in dragon boat races.

Overleaf: A brilliant sunset at the popular resort of Cable Beach, a few miles outside Broome.

facing death as punishment on deck; tales of treasure; and happily, a few tales of courage and survival.

With red pindan cliffs meeting the sky-blue sea, Broome is magnificent. The temperature is deliciously tropical, with a made-to-order sea breeze each afternoon. And to cap this storybook setting, the people are beautiful as well as exotic, the result of many races intermingling with the local Aboriginal people in the early pearling days. No wonder *Bran Nue Dae* was conceived here. Every day looks divinely created anew.

But all is not as idyllic as it once was. The Kimberley, with Broome as the gateway, was a frontier for the colonizers to conquer. And frontiers always attracted their fair share of cruel and amoral thrill-seekers. Callous slaughter of mobs of Aboriginal people and mass imprisonments of survivors, chained by the neck, was the norm. And not too many decades ago. Racism and attitudes of white superiority are still here and not far from the surface. There is no telling when they will show. It was two years ago that my wife, who is white, and I were enjoying a swim in the pool at one of the more prestigious resorts on the first day of a well-earned holiday. I was the only Aboriginal in the water, but blissfully unaware of this fact, until the manager loudly and rudely ordered me from the pool, refusing to believe I was a paying guest. It was embarrassing and uncomfortable, but certainly not the first time I have had to convince fellow Australians of my right to be granted admission, whether to restaurants, bars or taxis.

Small incidents like this can look as if they are of no real consequence, but such attitudes *en masse* make for some pretty sad business. In recent years, an all-white Broome jury acquitted two fellow white men of the brutal slaying of a young local Aboriginal boy, in spite of the fact that one of the men confessed and described in gruesome detail what he did to the victim.

Yet it is still possible to love this place, and to live a good life. The Aboriginal people in town have the hard task of lapping up each sun-filled day and looking forward to the next. And boy, they do enjoy themselves. Cheeky laughter, voices talking loud and fast, Broome-style, freshly caught fish frying on the barbecue – and maybe a turtle too if they have been really lucky. And of course music. It is everywhere the Aboriginals are, even if the guitar is a little makeshift or battered. People sing. They all join in, and know every word. Songs, fish, beer, good times, love, and a smattering of politics when they have to. Sigh! What a lifestyle.

The documentary producer and his assistant had done their homework and were dressed in khaki – a sensible move, even if they did look like they were straight off the *Out of Africa* movie set. And they had obviously been given the drum on the quintessential Australian bushman's headgear, the Akubra hat. I presume they wanted to blend in and look like one of the local mob, but they had made a fundamental error. Now, Akubra is the brand name of a type of hat made out of compressed rabbit pelts. It does not indicate a particular style. There's the dinky-di bushman style, and there's the embarrassing one you leave for the city cowboys – the pretenders – whose brim has turned-up sides like Americans wear. The Aussie style 'real blokes' favour is that of the cattle drover, which turns down low at the front. There's a practical reason for this snobbery. The cowboy shape sends the rain directly down your face or straight down the back of your neck, while the drover's shape is perfectly suited to our climate, shielding your face from both the scorching sun and the monsoon rains. My Pommy friends' hats screamed 'tourist' (or 'terrorist') to the locals. I felt for them, but enjoyed the fact that they were meeting all my expectations. I'd have hated it if they'd got it right.

We met our guide for the Kimberley interior here in Broome. Under Aboriginal law, respect must be shown both to the people who are custodians of the land, and to the land herself, by seeking permission and waiting to be shown through. There's no barrelling in just because you want to see the sights and feel it's your right to do so. The land, and the spirits, have ways of dealing with those who flout the law. Generally you will become sick until you realize your mistake and put it right. Our guide was Sam Lovell, accompanied by his wife Rosita, who was to be our cook. They are local Aboriginals who run a small tour operation called Outback Safaris, and would make sure we were granted safe passage through the traditional areas. Under my law I was to call him Uncle, out of respect for his knowledge and age. Uncle Sam is the sort of man who can colour darkness. He is the perfect guide, with a manner so calm and reassuring it is as if he has thrown a net of trust over you. We were in good hands.

With Auntie Rosita behind, driving the tucker truck, we set off along the Great Western Highway; our destination was Fitzroy Crossing. Heading inland is not something Australians do very often. We hug the coast. Since European settlement, white Australians have spoken of themselves as conquerors of the dry, hot inland – and yet all the major population centres are smack bang on the water's edge. But it's a very useful myth. I suppose you've got to think you can always head inland if things get pretty wonky in the world. If that day comes, I'm sure the indigenous blackfellas out there will be talked to in a pretty way then.

The red soil that the Kimberley is known for gave way to black. We were entering the silt-covered flood plains which dominate the landscape around the mighty Fitzroy River. It seems absurd that a land so parched is also the setting for regular and severe floods. Absurd or not, it happens, and the coast-hugging urban Australians annually gape in awe at our land of extremes. Exciting TV footage of foaming, rushing waters, dramatic overhead shots of stranded people and cattle, stories of Aboriginal communities totally cut off from all assistance and everybody pitching in to help, allow the city dwellers to share in the Australians' perception of themselves as a big-hearted, strong and resilient people. I'm not so sure we all fit the bill. However, to be fair, it's not often you get tested on such a scale in the suburbs.

Tall, red, strange-shaped termite mounds rose out of the black soil on both sides of the road. So many it was eerie and other-worldly. The locals call these plains the graveyards because of their cemetery-like appearance, but in fact the termites have always known a thing or two about survival. In their sun-resistant, air-conditioned dwellings they pack the sand so tightly that the station owners-cum-cattle barons used to roll the mounds flat to form a good solid surface for that old tribal game – tennis. Now to my mind, tennis is a pretty strange game to play out here, but I suppose it helped those poor fellas think they had even one small patch of red soil under control. And it appeals to my 'bushie's' sense of humour to think that such a refined creature provided the means for these strangers in their strange land to 'keep one's standards up'.

In fact it's a sense of humour which has helped us blackfellas through whatever European settlement has 'given' us. With a history which included a few massacres here, poisoned water-holes there, and the odd couple of thousand children forcibly taken away, a good laugh must surely be all that can lighten such a collective memory.

So when we veered sharp right off the highway in the dead of night, into thick pitch-black scrub in an attempt to find our proposed camping spot, the Fitzroy River bed, Uncle Sam and I were presented with the opportunity for a few laughs – but I'm not sure our humour was shared by our entourage. Sam particularly enjoyed the crew's sheer terror as we peeled ourselves off the ceiling on the roller-coaster-type incline to the river bed. 'Hang on' was all he had quietly suggested, as the car lights suddenly disappeared in front of us. His timing hinted that our comfort was not foremost in his mind – and anyway, scaring the living daylights out of our Pommy brethren is considered well within the rules. I also figured it was the right and proper thing for Uncle Sam to do.

The problem with any meeting of minds between polite but determined British, and polite, accommodating Aboriginal people is that the Aboriginal viewpoint can get stepped upon. The producer had kept us filming long past when any bushman knows camp should be set up – before the sun goes down. Uncle Sam just sat and waited, wondering at the driven behaviour of these *kartiya* (white people). No complaint. Just patiently taking it in.

We finally came to a halt on the flat wide river bed, where we set up camp by carlight. There was enough light to see the many exquisite patterns in the smooth river sand formed by the shifting waters. We made a fire and listened to the sounds of night birds and flying foxes. 'Not bad' is how we Aussies would describe it. Stunning is probably the word that someone from a more demonstrative race would choose. Tom, the photographer, decided a swim in the pure water was the ideal way to merge with such beauty. He was well prepared with a miner's hat – the perfect swimming accessory, I have always said – and we watched as the light beam went further and further away. It was time to tell him about a local Australian with an attitude problem – the good old crocodile. Tom's torch gained a life of its own, and was fairly swinging as he scanned every direction for those dreaded red eyes. Me – I was standing ankle deep enjoying the show, thinking he probably wouldn't listen right now if I explained the differences between the freshwater and saltwater varieties. 'Freshies', as they are known, are not as lethal as 'salties' – but it is always best to be sure. Breeding season can make them pretty stroppy. And anyway, Tom wasn't in the right frame of mind to work out which season it was. We knew he was okay, but I do wonder what kind of dreams he now has.

After breakfast we rounded up the troops and looked skyward at the way we had come in. It looked to be a 70-degree angle. Walking up and waiting became the most popular choice. With the benefit of daylight we could see that the roller-coaster dip was an actual road, one with deep potholes right next to large mounds of soil deposited by the many small creeks which head for the Fitzroy River any route they can after a rain. And when they do run, these creeks are tenacious. That big fella Rain is number-one boss up here, and the country bends, moves and grows in rapid response.

Fitzroy Crossing is visually jarring, especially in the middle of such beauty. Loads of empty beer cans litter each side of the road near the town fringes. Blackfellas wander aimlessly.

All Kimberley blackfellas were kicked off their own country by the station bosses when in 1965 Australian law said Aboriginal cattle workers were to be paid wages equivalent to the whites. They had no choice but to come here. Not only are they dispossessed, but different peoples (or tribes to the whitefellas) are now thrown together, regardless of historical taboos or whether those tribes have been enemies over the centuries. Traditional and cultural activities had to be virtually given up.

It's not surprising that trouble can come easily. So can a sense of futility. But what are they to do? There are no jobs for them, and they are denied access to their lands. They are also confronted daily with a particularly attractive brand of Australian – the redneck. Pastoralists talk of taking up arms if government legislation decrees that traditional lands must be given back. Some station owners are more blatant and take pot-shots.

One black brother described Fitzroy Crossing as being like a dartboard – whitefellas in the middle, and blackfellas all around. The only problem with this analogy is that here all the targets are on the outer rim. The town whites, who live in the almost exclusively white centre of town, don't talk to the 'black' blackfellas, who live on the fringes, and who wander shamelessly (in white eyes) through town. Fair-skinned blackfellas have the dubious privilege of being 'liked' by the *kartiya*.

An unnecessarily large police force never seems to stop cruising, and on race day the jails are overflowing. The streets have to look nice for visitors.

As we drove in, I thought of the old 'black bar' with its cement floor and mesh wire around the counter, which made you think you were in a cattle yard. The white lounge bar opposite taunted the black patrons with its carpeted areas, its mixed drinks, cold beer in real glasses, and the prospect of playing pool in comfort. But all is not gloomy. Progress has hit Fitzroy Crossing. The wire was removed four years ago. However, the black bar is still there, ironically with the pub now owned by blackfellas and run for them by white management. Something sounds wrong here – but hey, I'm only a visitor.

To a whitefella, the strangest thing about this town must be that the blackfellas will tell you with absolute conviction they love it. 'It's deadly,' was how my mate who used the

*The rugged outlines of the boab trees are common in the
Kimberley. They are closely related to the African boabab,
and their ancestors may have arrived in Australia as seeds which
floated thousands of miles across the Indian Ocean.*

*Opposite: Crossing the dry bed of the Fitzroy River
on the Great Western Highway.*

Overleaf: Gum trees on the river bank at Fitzroy Crossing.

dartboard analogy described it. But he wasn't meaning you might lose your life, even though that didn't seem far from the truth. He was using the local Aboriginal lingo in which 'deadly' means the best there could possibly be. 'That *kartiya* can take it away, but we will always go back,' said my mate, 'because it's [my] country. To him it's just a possession. To us it's everything.'

There are two pubs in tiny Fitzroy, and we camped at the flash one. My notes tell me the rednecks must have been out in force, but I only know this because, when I sat down to write after I was back home in Sydney, I came across a list of questions my producer wanted me to address. 'How do you feel about the racist comments we witnessed?' he had written. I don't remember them. Over the years I suppose I have learnt to tune out. You have to in Australia. Otherwise you would be immobilized by sadness. My wife is frequently asked how her family reacted when she married an Aboriginal.

I was impressed with the flash pub. It had been sensibly built on stilts to cope with the annual flood threat. However, the location, a small patch of raised ground wedged in between two flood plains, didn't really suggest an absolute safe haven. But the stilts were a thoughtful touch, I mused, as I peered below. When the water rose you could watch your car being swept away from right under your feet.

The trucks were loaded, and Uncle Sam quietly gave the true cattleman's catch-cry, 'Move 'em out!' I was a staunch Audie Murphy fan when I was a kid. Anybody who can talk like a cowboy is a king to me still. I could almost smell the cattle every time Uncle Sam said it. And he said it as if it were a ritual. He'd been a cattleman for most of his life, and it's in his blood. We were on the road again, heading further inland, this time to one of the few remaining privately owned cattle stations, Fossil Downs.

You can't come to the Kimberley without visiting a station. The legendary feats of the Kimberley cattlemen feature heavily in the Australian psyche. There are many stories of the first Europeans droving big mobs of cattle across thousands of miles of uncharted and unforgiving country, opening up stock routes and looking for land on which to establish their stations. It is stirring stuff, full of high adventure. Nowadays everyone would like to be as manly as those drovers and station hands were believed to be. How do I know this? Just walk down some of the ritziest streets in Sydney or Melbourne, and start counting those city boys in the cattleman's 'uniform' – riding boots, moleskins and Driza-Bones, the famous Aussie oilskin coat.

Only trouble with all this legend-making and land-finding is that, contrary to popular belief, they were not the first. There were already people living there, people who knew how to handle the harsh climate, who didn't find the land unforgiving and unyielding, and who had travelled those routes many times themselves, on foot. And under their law they

*Stockmen from the cattle stations show off their skills
in a local rodeo.*

61

had been assigned custodial rights to the same land claimed by the white men. Just a few oversights by those whitefella historians and myth-makers. They can be a little colour-blind sometimes.

There are mixed feelings about the cattle industry among Aboriginal people. Ever since the horse and the cattle first came (the polite way the old people refer to the white man), Aboriginal people had worked on the stations. Originally most had been forced – rounded up by the police and delivered to the station managers when they requested more labour. Any resistance resulted in a bullet. And killings were a-plenty if they attempted to escape back to their country. Aboriginal stockmen today still remember seeing family and friends shot and killed at the whim of the station managers. This was truly Australia's Wild West.

The Aboriginal people who worked alongside white men were often in charge because of their adeptness and skill. For their labour they were allocated rations of tea, tobacco, sugar and a blanket, while the white men were paid a good wage plus keep. When things got better for the blackfellas they were ever so generously given a pair of boots and a set of clothing. Today, the Kimberley Aboriginal people believe it was the free (or arguably slave) labour which built the cattle industry here. 'But we were only good enough to work without money,' said a mate back at Fitzroy Crossing. It hurts now to be almost excluded, ironically since the introduction of the award wage which was introduced with the intention of giving the Aboriginal workers a fair go. Instead it merely highlighted the station bosses preference to hire, and pay, white workers over Aboriginal.

There are those who grew to love the station work, probably due to the fair go they were given by some decent and humane station managers. They are still spoken of with great respect. Many Aboriginal stockmen still hunger for a good muster and the chance to use their skills again. They gaze with sad eyes at the eroded soil, and shake their heads with disbelief at the exhausted and bruised cattle now mustered furiously, and sometimes until death, by helicopter instead of the old, gentler way by men on horseback.

The industry no longer flourishes. Most stations are now in the hands of large companies, out to make the quickest buck they can for their shareholders. Helicopter mustering is one of the destructive cost-effective methods ordered by city board members, whose only consideration is profit, certainly not people or the land.

Fossil Downs at least is still privately owned, and by people who love the country. Uncle Sam had been the manager of a nearby station, and knew the Fossil Downs owners well. They were respected. They had treated their Aboriginal workers fairly – although, like all the stations, they had followed the tea, sugar and tobacco payment method in earlier times.

Out of the powder-fine bulldust we swung through the gates, past the incongruous Scottish crest on the stone fence. Was I dreaming? I looked up and saw green on green – with palm trees – in a well-kept garden. Where did this come from? I couldn't help wondering if they had a termite mound surface on their tennis court.

*Le Lievre's Western Outfitters: a travelling shop opens
for business at Fitzroy Crossing.*

Annette Henwood, a granddaughter of the Macdonalds who first established the station, graciously served us tea in the garden. The Poms might have expected some ill feeling on my part, because my early years had been spent on a station in circumstances typical of all Aboriginal people of that time, and in stark contrast to the wealth on display here. My mother had been a kitchenhand.

But she had taught me well, and resentment or ill feeling was not on the list. What Annette had was fine. Her family had created it, and they had done so without the excesses the Kimberley *kartiya* were known for.

What I was interested in was the fact that, even with all this opulence – by my standards anyway – there is no escape in the Kimberley from dancing to the tune the rain plays when it comes. The house had been designed specifically so that the floodwaters would part and cause minimal impact. And the billiard table in the sumptuous games room was on a winch pulley to be lifted safely above the water line. You've got to be prepared for anything out here, no matter who you are or what your bank balance. And it looked like they were – just like everybody else.

There aren't too many roads in this part of Australia, and to get to our next destination we backtracked through Fitzroy Crossing, then headed north. My goodness, bitumen. Oh yes. For the tourists. I missed the fine bulldust spraying everywhere. What is a trip in this part of the country if you don't end up with a red sheen and coated nostrils?

We head for Geikie Gorge, a popular tourist haunt, to meet an old mate of mine, Joe Ross, an Aboriginal ranger with CALM – Conservation and Land Management. He is to take us by boat up the Fitzroy River to where it crosses the Geikie Range forming a spectacular gorge. We're going a bit further than the white rangers take the white tourists.

The Aboriginal rangers take you on a journey that is more than just lunch with a bit of look-see thrown in. Their tour is look with a heap of feel and know. And they take you with the blessings of the Aboriginal elders whose decision it was to allow some of their mysteries to be shown. Maybe they were thinking, 'We've got to help those poor old whitefellas somehow.'

It takes time for those whitefellas to see what's right in front of their eyes, and they couldn't seem to see the blackfellas up here for quite a while, except as target practice. They have only been given jobs as rangers in recent years, but surely they were always the obvious choice. Joe and the other Aboriginal rangers know this land. They belong here. Joe's mother is a tribal woman from the area, and his father a larger-than-life white man who has lived here, with the Aboriginal people, since he was a boy.

In Aboriginal law, traditional custodians have always been appointed to make sure the land was given what she needed, and was treated with the reverence and respect due her. When the white man came he spread those cattle and sheep to roam over millions of acres, without measures to protect and nurture her. She became merely the means to create wealth. Gratitude was a concept reserved for people – certainly not for a patch of dirt, a few

Ernie and Sam hit the road for Geikie Gorge.

scraggy old trees and those nuisance rocks which were no good as cattle country. I have a theory, far-fetched as it may be, that the massive soil erosion and degradation on most of the grazing areas is the Kimberley plotting to get rid of the white man, so she can resurrect herself. Who knows, in this ancient land of the Creator. It will take a few years, I suppose, but the land is as patient as the old people here. And time is on her side.

At least now, in the cattle-free National Parks, the Aboriginal rangers can either maintain the Kimberley as she is, or put things right. It's a step in the right direction. Joe and the other Aboriginal rangers act as mediators between the traditional people and the Conservation and Land Management, and advise how the old ways can be implemented. A lot of listening is what they ask.

Joe is like most Aboriginal people raised with the benefit of traditional knowledge. Like Uncle Sam, he is calm and sure and is not one for small talk. They leave that to the whitefellas who by their constant chatter seem to be frantically trying to find something, anything which will give a base to their lives. Endless instructions and questions for the documentary are brushed aside or not answered. Poor old whitefellas. Silence seems to scare them. Blackfellas of the bush don't have that fear. And blackfellas who have been in the city too long – that's me – have to be taught all over again. Maybe that's why I was taken back. To learn to listen to the silence. There's plenty of it here.

Up the river we went in our flat-bottomed boat, through the majesty of Geikie Gorge. The gorge is about 350 million years old, give or take a few million, according to Joe. Ancient black fossils form layer upon layer, overlaid with a white flood mark. Green trees. White ghost gums. Blue skies. Occasional birds. The rhythmic sound of the motor punching upstream. And crocodiles. Lots. 'A bit of all right' is the Aussie expression which comes to mind.

'This is a Dreamtime place here,' Joe said simply, when we arrived at the special pool he was taking us to. 'Mangunambi. Bunuba name for this place.' The name Mangunambi is full of beauty when pronounced correctly, in the quick singing style it should be. It loses its charm when whitefellas draw the syllables out, stressing every letter. We've got a lot of educating to do.

And Joe's simple sentences said many things for those who already have the right education. They spoke of a connection which ties each of the Bunuba people, whose country this is, to each of their ancestors, grandfather to grandfather, grandmother to grandmother, in one long line back to the time of the Dreaming when beings first came. They also tell of the interconnectedness of all the different Aboriginal peoples. Same Dreamings, different names with each people.

With Joe Ross, their Aboriginal ranger guide, Ernie and Sam
explore the spectacular gorge where the Fitzroy River crosses
the Geikie Range.

Connections are what give the Aboriginal people their life. They know with certainty how they are connected to, and a part of, everything which surrounds them. Stories connect, families connect. It is so complex that whitefellas often give up trying to understand, or just dismiss the culture as primitive. Animals and plants connect as well. Nothing lives in isolation. A blackfella in his own 'country' knows, therefore, how he is an actual part of the universe. He does not suffer the loneliness that whitefellas force on themselves. (Maybe that's why we always say 'Poor whitefellas'.) Through the Dreamtime, and the stories of Creation, he knows he is the rocks, the trees, animals and the land. A blackfella whose Dreaming (or spirit or totem) is a kangaroo or a honey-ant for instance, would never eat one because he would be eating himself.

Joe told us that the pool, a natural spring, is the eye of the water python, the rainbow serpent. It is a very powerful place, and is only one part of the Dreamtime story for Geikie Gorge. As part of the initiation ceremonies of the Bunuba people, all young boys of a certain age are thrown into the water. Their spirits travel to the other side, and they come out as men. Boyhood has been left behind. A big corroboree, with all the women and those who have been waiting, is held on the side where they emerge. It is a time of great celebration for who they have become, and an honouring of the life-giving force which resides there.

At 'ceremony time' each year this pool and the area around it are out of bounds. This is no lightweight occasion, but one of the strands of the complex web which must be observed. The full ceremony is known only to the initiated ones, and is kept secret. To witness a ceremony without permission is to invite trouble from the spirits of the land, and you will pay dearly, sometimes with your life. The pool, and the water python whose eye this is, knows who is worthy and who is not. Since whitefellas first came to our country they have dismissed all this as just superstition. The state of their health after an unauthorized visit tells the truth.

Joe took us to meet his father, Peter, one of the all-time decent men. I could hear him long before he came into view. He's what is always referred to as a 'character' – larger than life, a bit gruff and with a heart as big as Australia. We sat yarning around a campfire, and he had plenty to tell. An orphan who was sent from England as a boy, he has devoted his time to the local Aboriginal people. He told how, back in the fifties, there had been a bad drought, and he had been 'conned' into doing some water-boring, working with a blackfella. 'It was that bloke who taught me how to water-bore,' he said. 'I got a pound a foot, and he got nothing. We've learned at the expense of the poor blackfella.' It's blokes like Peter who will help to put it right.

Uncle Sam didn't say 'Move 'em out!' this time. Something was wrong. Auntie Rosita knew it, and I knew it. We felt bad, and we felt for Uncle Sam. He had let some information slip, and the producer suggested that Sam's story was a good one to tell. Like tens of thousands of other Aboriginal children of mixed blood, he had been forcibly taken from his full-descent mother when he was a boy. It is a story which should be told, as yet another shameful part of Australia's white history. But not this way, not for the camera.

It was a case of the European not understanding the huge cultural differences between themselves and the Aboriginal people. White Australians are guilty of it every day. Uncle Sam was asked to relive the immeasurable sorrow he had managed to suppress and traditional Aboriginal culture does not permit a 'no' answer. It is considered extremely impolite and hurtful. The old ways of relaying the idea of 'no' without actually saying it, such as deflection, changing the subject or simply not answering, rely on everybody understanding the rules. The producer didn't. Not many whitefellas do. So the polite but determined once again held sway over the polite and accommodating. Uncle Sam did not wish to offend, and was quietly grieving.

At first, when the children were taken away, they were rounded up by police on horseback. Babies were sometimes ripped from their mother's arms. As the state became more 'civilized' representatives from Native Welfare would call. Some station managers, who had frequently fathered the children, would arrange for the Aboriginal men to be working several days' journey away. Children were scooped from under beds, or from the bushes where the families were desperately trying to hide them. The blackfellas were rarely successful. The *kartiya* came again and again. Families wailed and never forgot their children, and in turn the children never forgot where they had come from.

Uncle Sam finally found his mother many years later. He wasn't meant to find her again – indeed, he was never meant to want to. Official government policy was to make him identify with the white blood in his veins, far away from the influence of his people who, it was hoped, would all die out. It didn't work.

The producer arranged for Sam to take us to his birthplace. He hadn't been there for over thirty years. I will skip the details. Uncle Sam is not a curiosity. He is a man who still feels deep sorrow, like the many thousands in Australia whose lives have been carbon copies of his. When we arrived he answered questions with no enthusiasm, and finally pulled his hat over his eyes while he cried. I felt great shame for my part in bringing his pain to the surface. I would have been honoured to have been taken to his birthplace under different circumstances. As it was, I was pleased to leave.

All this stuff can get to a bloke if you let it. We needed to see some heroes. Blackfella heroes. If the story of the Kimberley and Australia is not told correctly, it can sound like the blackfella just lay down and said 'Step on me'. Not so. There were many heroes, and many, many brave men who died resolutely as their warriorhood had trained them, facing the *kartiya* who were on horseback carrying guns, while they were on foot, armed with just a few wooden spears, a woomera (spear-thrower) and a shield. Those stories haven't made it into the white history books yet.

Uncle Sam took us to Jandamarra's country. A Bunuba man, Jandamarra lived at the end of the nineteenth century. He died then also, but he led the whitefellas such a merry chase for so long, and he was said to have such miraculous powers, that the cattlemen asked for proof that he was dead. Only then could they confidently go back on to his tribal homeland and claim it as theirs. He had jeopardized the expansion of the sheep and cattle industry, and had to be destroyed. His head was severed from his body and displayed in Derby, on the coast, before being pickled and sent to England. There was no shame for him in this. The shame belonged totally to the whitefellas.

Jandamarra was known to the *kartiya* as Pigeon because he was small and fast. He was a black tracker for the police. His job? To track Aboriginal 'troublemakers'. Mostly trackers were forced into this role. Their families were threatened if they tried to say no. The men themselves were flogged. And if they still refused they were shot. Not much choice. There never was. Most were taken far away from their homelands and never made it back. At first Jandamarra, like all trackers, was used against other tribes. The biggest mistake the police made was to try to force him to betray his own people. Seventeen Bunuba elders, respected initiated law-men, were chained together at the neck and feet to a tree at Lillimiloora police station. They had been rounded up because a few sheep had been stolen from the station established on their tribal lands. Jandamarra helped them escape, and in the process shot and killed a policeman. He then became a fugitive.

Aboriginal people have never forgotten his fight, which lasted over three years. As he evaded capture against all the odds – and many determined whitefellas – the legend grew. To them he became a revered symbol of resistance. To the whitefellas, a pest to exterminate.

Lillimiloora is now the first stop for tourists on the Pigeon Heritage Trail. The elderly white coach travellers look at the scenery and wonder why they are there. Most Australians do not know of the massacres and inhuman treatment of Aboriginal people (in fact most Australians have not met an Aboriginal and do not go out of their way to do so). It hardly rates a mention in schools even now, and certainly didn't a few years ago. The school system used to teach the line that they were going to die out anyway. And how benevolent the state was to round up the improved version – that is, those with white blood. Then they could at least be made useful as housemaids, cooks and rouseabouts. Never on an equal footing with the whitefella, though, because they were genetically inferior.

The tourists do not come here to have their version of history overturned. You can't blame them. They are on holiday, and want to enjoy the scenery and relax. Besides, with their belief systems firmly established and in agreement with the majority of Australians, how could they possibly understand Jandamarra's fight? The coach drivers know why it's important. It helpfully provides a story around which they base a day trip. Lunch is the highlight, of course.

The next stop in Jandamarra's story, and therefore also on the coach trips, is Windjana Gorge, where the river has cut through the ancient coral reef in a spectacular fashion to create sheer cliffs. They go straight up and are surely impossible to climb. In one shoot-out, the white stockmen and police covered both ends of the gorge, trapping Jandamarra. They went in for the kill, but found only the women who had acted as decoys. Jandamarra and

Ernie and Sam inside the great network of caves at Tunnel Creek, where the Aboriginal tracker Jandamarra hid out for years from his white kartiya *hunters.*

the men had gone over the top. There are stories of him running effortlessly over the jagged coral in his bare feet, while the *kartiya's* leather boots were ripped to pieces.

This was his country and she sheltered him. For three years he used Tunnel Creek, a massive, winding cave system over half a mile long, as a hiding place. Only his wife and mother knew where he was. When the *kartiya* came looking, he would fire the two guns he had set up, one for each entrance, then escape through shafts of whose existence they had no idea. When we came looking, the *kartiya* assistant nearly found her own hiding place – for ever. In the pitch black, cut only by our high-powered torches, we waded through deep freezing water (Jandamarra's living quarters were not particularly comfortable). I'm 6 feet 3 inches (1.9 metres). The assistant, a 'shorty', was behind me as we filed through, feeling our way and pushing against the water. Splash, splash – and over my shoulder a head started bobbing, arms and legs frantically dog-paddling.

Comfortable the quarters were not, but beautiful they most certainly were. Ancient paintings on the ceiling. Stalactites and stalagmites. It looked like a castle for fairies. Jandamarra had his own look-out high up in the darkness where he slept, and off that another small cave. There were stories that his miraculous powers prevented bullets harming him. It was here he would come and wait for their wounds to heal, while his mother and wife brought food.

Dingo Gap was where he died, having dragged himself there, bleeding profusely from three bullets embedded in his body as he tried to get back to Tunnel Creek. Aboriginal trackers from another tribe led the police to him. The Gap is beautiful from a distance. But when there – well, it's a sad place. Jandamarra had died on his own, tracked by Aboriginal people. I needed some quiet time. Uncle Sam understood.

There are questions in Kimberley blackfella minds about what really happened out there. The police claimed Jandamarra was finally killed by a rifle shot to the head at close range. They were standing over him. Would much of his skull still have been intact? Many think not. Was it really Jandamarra's head they displayed in Derby? Or did they kill another poor blackfella just to have a head, any head, on display to placate the station owners and the authorities. The white tourists are not given this information to ponder.

We restocked, ready for a solid three-day drive to Kalumburu mission, way up north. We left Derby and rattled up the corrugation known as the Gibb River Road, heading into what was unknown territory to me. We would be travelling through traditional country and I needed permission from the custodians. To get this, Uncle Sam and I went ahead of the film crew. I'd never been this far up before, and I was feeling lost and even a little afraid. Uncle Sam sensed this and reassured me, in the way all traditional blackfellas have of addressing an issue without actually mentioning it. 'Funny road up in here,' he said. 'Been all through this country mustering cattle, from down that way, up through there

Ernie and Sam looking down on Dingo Gap.

and back across again so many times.' He would look out for me. He knew the country. I needn't worry.

Asking permission is done in the same indirect way. To whitefellas it can be totally confusing. In fact they think nothing of consequence has happened. It's all in the interpretation of what is said and not said. No direct question or reply is allowed. Both are considered rude. A 'no' answer may sometimes need to be given, and neither party wants to offend the other by doing so. Each must know what the answer is without the actual words being spoken.

When we stopped at the Aboriginal outstation, what sounded like very easy, general conversation took place. 'He's heading up this way doing a fillum with these England fullas,' said Uncle Sam as he introduced me, altering his speech to fit the traditional elders' English language skills.

'Hm,' they sang. 'We see you on the television.' They knew who I was. 'And how long you stayin' up this way?' More slow conversation, then, 'Which way you goin'?' and 'When you headin' back that way?' Finally, 'When you get up to Mount Barnett, say hello to that Billy King for me.' Permission had been granted, and Billy King was now responsible for ensuring our safety.

We stayed over at Mount Barnett, where Billy King was. Mount Barnett is a station leased in 1987 by the government to the Gupingarri people. The community is thriving, and they have increased their head of cattle from just eight hundred to over two thousand. It was so good to see blackfellas doing what they know and love. On their land. We had to go mustering. Uncle Sam was after a chance to say 'Move 'em out!' in the right setting.

The Aboriginal stockmen have worked with and nurtured the cattle since they were calves. When they are old enough and it is time to move them, all the stockmen need do is give a gentle nudge and the cattle respond. So different from the frenetic and cruel helicopter mustering on the large company-owned stations. We were rolling along, feeling like cattle kings, when the cattle became a little stir-crazy. A helicopter to take aerial shots for the documentary was whirring close overhead, and the cattle shot through in all directions. They were frightened. I felt responsible. We had brought the very thing the men had sought to avoid. The patient stockmen calmed the cattle and thought no more about it.

After a long drive through the sparse country, we finally arrived at Kalumburu in the early evening when the sun was low. It was a beautiful sight. An oasis in the middle of nowhere, bathed in an orange glow. A silver water tank stood high above the buildings. The fences fought to hold back the orchard. There was a feeling of richness, of abundance. The land was bursting with life. There was something happening here which pleased her.

Kalumburu had been established earlier this century, as a Catholic mission to bring Christianity to the Aboriginal people. It no longer operated as one and is now run by the Aboriginal people, although there was no mistaking a church presence still. A number of nuns, complete with habits, could be seen going about their duties.

It was Sunday and the evening church service was scheduled. The congregation consisted of about thirty blackfellas and four whitefellas. The Father had obviously taken to the tropical lifestyle, and conducted the service dressed in a loose shirt, gym boots and shorts. Some of the blackfellas, by contrast, were spruced right up, especially the kids. Frills even. And white dresses. They got the day right for Sunday-best.

The Aboriginal missions have had bad press over the years, and they do not fit with my beliefs. However, there are many old blackfellas who state with conviction that, if the missions hadn't been in the Kimberley, all the Aboriginal people would have been wiped out. When the police and cattlemen were shooting to exterminate the bushmen, the only ones saved, they claim, were the refugees who came to the missions.

Here, now, the culture of the local mob is undergoing a resurgence. The old people, men and women, go into the school and teach the kids, both black and white. When we were there, there was a mock-up corroboree as part of the school curriculum. Each child had a little lap-lap or loincloth (with their names on so they wouldn't lose it), and each was painted up by the old people, who sang traditional songs as they did so. The kids danced, and the old men sang and shouted instructions. The women also sang along and encouraged everyone to participate. There was a lot of laughter. The songs told of survival, and of enjoying life. The kids didn't look as if they needed to be taught much about that. In the dance simply called 'shake-a-leg', the red dirt flew. Their little legs were hammering ten to the dozen. The traditional culture was safe here. It would continue to be passed down. I suspect this is why the land was happy.

The producer had arranged for Uncle Sam and Auntie Rosita to leave us and drive back to Broome. I was to continue down the coast by sea plane, joining up with a pearling lugger and doing a spot of ooh-ing and aah-ing over the huge and stunning Paspaley South Sea pearls. I did just that. The coastline was spectacular: the sunrise, pearls, the turtles, dolphins, even a whale and her calf, and then the sunset, were a joy to behold. But my heart wasn't in it. My journey had ended when Uncle Sam, with his calm, patient ways, left. I felt incomplete and alone. Alone amongst the *kartiya* and the Poms. And anyway, I am freshwater, from freshwater people, not saltwater. I have no connection with this country. More importantly, no Aboriginal people knew I was travelling out here, and I no longer had anybody to look out for me. It is not the Aboriginal way to travel alone.

Back in Broome, I knew the land was sending me home. It was time. I felt a little strange. There was a dreamy calmness I hadn't had before. The soul of the Earth had done her work. I now had mine to do. I had seen her magnificence and her plight. Funny how this trip had turned into an unofficial history destined for the world.

My old grandfather used to say, 'You've got two ears and one mouth for a good reason. You should listen twice as much as you speak.' Well, all these whitefellas have been doing a mighty lot of speaking, and not much listening. And so had I. Time to put things right.

THE CARIBBEAN
Tony Robinson

I have never been particularly good at pleasure. I'm great at having a nice time, but 'pleasure' – the word's always reminded me of one of those thick, treacly, English steamed puddings; the sort of thing that's quite tasty while you're shovelling it down, but afterwards you put on weight, and feel guilty and a bit sick. I've had my moments of shovelling obviously, but generally I'm more ant than grasshopper.

Except that now I'd decided to give it a go. The Big Five Zero was hurtling towards me like a rusty guillotine blade. If I didn't party now, I never would, would I? I was going to embark on a hedonistic journey through the senses. I was going to stuff myself so full of pleasure that, by the time I'd finished, it would be leaking out of my ears. And where would I find it? Well, it had to be the West Indies, didn't it!

Kingston, Jamaica

Louise was one of the most daunting people I've ever met. She was big, with a wall eye, her hands were twisted and scarred, and she was vitriolically angry – angry at imperialism, angry at colonialism, very angry at white men. I'd better watch my step, she said. She knew what people like me were like. Did I realize that the government was hell bent on closing Jamaican Dance Hall down, just as it always tried to gag the authentic voice of the people? If I really wanted a chance to see what Dance Hall was all about I'd better not bad-mouth her people or trivialize her arguments, OK? I swore I wouldn't. Why on earth should I?

Palm trees and blue skies on a paradise island - Dominica.

77

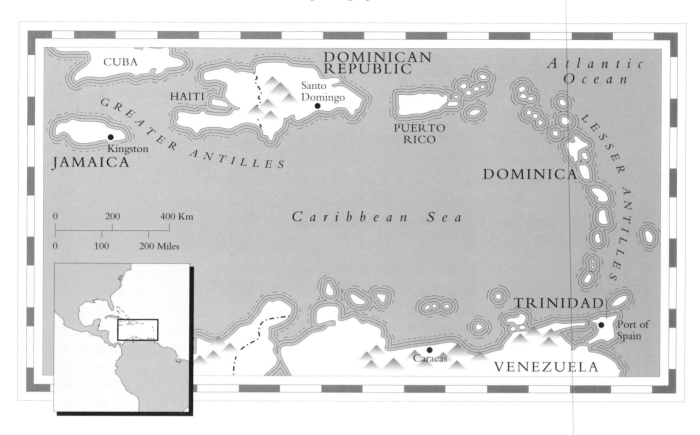

We drove for about an hour to a suburb that reminded me of Dagenham. In the shelter of a dusty, redundant quarry lay the dance hall. At the entrance I was frisked for bottles, knives and drugs, and felt a wave of homesickness. It was just like getting into the football back home. I'm great at conjuring up Third World stereotypes, so obviously I expected the place to be shabby and run-down. But it wasn't – it was spick and span (is anything spick without being span, I wonder?), and painted in dazzling Caribbean pinks and greens – 'like the inside of a cabbage', someone murmured, but I think the ganja had got to her.

I was the only white person among a thousand hot black bodies, swaying expectantly, singing gently along to brief bursts of reggae, a patchwork of extracts from the hits of the last five years. 'Kill the Batty Boy! Kill the Batty Boy!' chanted the crowd, punctuated by a disembodied voice yelling 'ROOYYY!', all low and gravelly, then 'LIGHTER! LIGHTER, LIGHTER!' What did 'lighter' mean? That we should sing more softly? That the owner of the voice required a flat-bottomed barge? I didn't know.

Then a roar broke out as the night's big star burst on to the tiny stage. This was the wicked boy himself, he told us, 'The Selector, the Number One International DJ in the Whole of Jamaica – Skyjuice!!' He was fantastic. He strutted, he crowed, he ripped his shirt off and wobbled his belly. And when he yelled 'Lighter!' again, a hundred Dunhills and Ronsons flared into the air. It was a sophisticated nineties' version of the little hippy ceremony I'd first encountered when Leonard Cohen was droning on at the Isle of Wight

78

Festival in nineteen-sixty-whatever-it-was. Only whereas in those days we burned our fingers on pathetic little paper matches, these flames were sophisticated gas, flicking on and off in time to the music like stoned fireflies.

'I want four good girls to get up on the stage right now,' chanted Skyjuice. 'There's a hundred Jamaican dollars right here for the little miss who can really skin up, really shake her little booty and drive us wild!' This was what I'd been waiting for – a moment of genuine communal pleasure ... a contemporary counter-culture bursting with freshness, sensuality and innovation ... a slap in the face for the forces of state morality. May '68 wasn't dead. It lived on in the hearts and bodies of the young Kingston girls who, in exchange for the Jamaican equivalent of £2.50, would drown their misery in an un-inhibited display of adolescent sensuality. Well, that's what I'd been expecting. That's what I thought Louise had laid on for me.

Four round-shouldered, stony-faced young women, dressed in see-through body stockings, G-strings and Lurex, clambered on to the stage and began to gyrate. They looked about as committed to job satisfaction as King's Cross hookers. After ten minutes of tired pelvic aerobics, they slouched off back into the shadows. I was gutted.

Where was Louise? I could have been doing something useful tonight, like sleeping off my jet lag. She'd promised me roots: why had she delivered only sleaze?

At worst I was expecting a grudging apology, at best that she'd take me somewhere else where the dancing was everything she'd cracked it up to be. Instead, I was flattened by Hurricane Louise. She represented the Jamaican Musicians' Union, she said. There was no way she was going to allow nice, ordinary Kingston girls up on that stage while some writer from England was watching. I'd seen four professional dancers – what more did I want? And anyway, I hadn't paid her enough; and did I realize that the government had rung her up this very morning to say they'd banned the sort of dancing I'd asked to see? Obviously I wanted to get her into trouble. She'd realized that the moment I'd walked through her door.

'So why did you offer to bring me here?' I asked in that reasonable tone of voice I usually reserve for traffic wardens and VAT inspectors. But it was no use. Louise had made up her mind. I wasn't going to witness any unalloyed pleasure tonight, and that was that.

I wandered back inside again. On stage, three adolescent boys were rapping a Joycean stream of braggadocio. They were expressing the sort of sentiments that you shouldn't divulge to anyone except your therapist, who's paid to hear such things without concluding you're a complete git. There was a burst of applause, then the disco started up again. 'Kill the Batty Boy! Kill the Batty Boy!' went Skyjuice, and once again the audience joined in the refrain.

I got a cab back to the hotel thinking that, for all her bluster, Louise had probably been pretty shrewd. It was best that I was kept away from Dance Hall. I'd loved the crowd, I'd loved their energy, I'd loved the way the audience participation was the show itself. But I'd left feeling pretty uneasy. 'Batty Boy' is Jamaican slang for 'gay'. I'd just witnessed a whole hall full of people baying for the death of the homosexuals in their community. It was a bit chilling.

Before I'd left, Louise had treated me to a final tirade. Satellites and TV stations have imported a moral degeneracy into the Caribbean, she'd said. What I'd heard was justified because it was an attack by disempowered youth on the corrupt basis of US imperialism. Well, Louise, the problem with that argument is that it's … bollocks!

You see, she was right. I am just another white person who bad-mouthed her people and trivialized her arguments.

Port of Spain, Trinidad

OK. I'll come clean. The main reason I haven't dedicated my life to the pursuit of pleasure is guilt. I don't have the same problem with the pursuit of pain. I can suffer bereavement, the sack, humiliating put-downs from beautiful women, amputation and a whole jawful of root canal fillings, and stoically put it down to some mysterious divine plan, but give me a few moments' uninterrupted pleasure and I start panicking. 'I shouldn't be doing this,' I think, 'it's not improving me. I'll go and be creative. Sort out the paper clips, maybe, or cut my toenails.'

I blame Christianity. Well, not Jesus – he's always seemed a pretty sound guy. It's Paul who's the problem – what a grouchy, misogynous old killjoy he was. You think you have a problem with guilt? Imagine if you'd been a gay vicar in the church at Corinth when zealot Paul was the bishop. Why did he have to go and invent Christianity? If he'd left it to Jesus we'd have ended up with a much nicer religion.

I was mulling over all this while contemplating the scenery and being served home-made lemonade by a pair of monks. The monastery of Mount Benedict, high above Port of Spain, has a spectacular view over Trinidad. In fact it's so spellbinding I was surprised the abbot hadn't erected sight screens so the monks could concentrate on their inner life without distraction.

The abbot was vastly tall, with a grizzly beard and craggy face, like the loopy one in *The Name of the Rose*. The two monks were less daunting. Brother Gerard, the sports teacher, had joined the order straight from school forty years ago and looked like he'd kept a straight bat ever since. And as for Father John (bright, intellectual, recently appointed monastery novice-master), I reckoned he was a racing certainty for Pope by the end of the century – either that or excommunication.

'Doesn't Paul's fanatical disapproval of the things of the flesh seem pretty dysfunctional compared to the sensual Jesus of the Gospels?' I asked them. The abbot said that as far as the Early Christians were concerned, the end of the world really was nigh. So for Paul, carnality was a stupid distraction, given that everyone was going to be plunged into the fires of Hell before the end of the tax year. His answer seemed to prove my point. If my number was up, the first thing I'd do would be to reach for my corkscrew, my address book and a packet of Rizlas. On second thoughts I probably wouldn't … I'd feel too damned guilty.

By now the conversation was really humming. Father John was passionately defending the concept of Carnival – the mainstay of Trinidad's cultural life. In the midst of pleasure you can touch God, he was saying. There's a deep creativity in Carnival. For two whole days every year the islanders share a solidarity, a unity, a celebration of artistic activity and multi-ethnicity … a holiness.

The abbot wasn't having any of this. He told us lurid stories about innocent women in the Carnival crowd having their behinds rubbed by the private parts of unknown men, about a calypso singer who played with herself while singing of the pleasures of the Carnival bacchanal. If he hadn't been a man of the cloth, I could have sworn the abbot was getting a little heated. He told us of a girl who'd come to him in distress. She'd recently found God, but now she'd been asked to dress up as the Devil for tomorrow's Carnival, and though she didn't want to let her friends down, she found the idea of being Satan obscene. So the abbot had counselled her to wear the Devil's costume but to leave the horns and tail at home – advice which seemed to me pretty consistent with Church policy since the days of Paul.

I'd expected Brother Gerard to say nothing, but suddenly he leaped in too. The exciting thing about Carnival, he said, was that it allowed anyone to be anything they chose. For centuries the people of the West Indies had been slaves, the women prostituted, the men tortured and killed – as a nation they had a problem finding a new identity, as individuals it was hard to feel self-respect. Carnival liberated the soul – for its duration you could be a king, a general, a demi-god, and nobody would say you nay.

Father John was really pumping gas now. If only church services were more like Carnival, he said. That's what it had been like when the Pope came to the West Indies – non-stop parties, calypso and steel bands. The Catholic service is based on celebratory music and art from another century and another culture. It's time to recreate the Church as an expression of the joys and pleasures that people find in their lives today – that would be genuine worship.

I really liked Father John. He had that irresistible combination of passion and intelligence which I'm sure will draw him to the attention of the Church authorities. I hope promotion doesn't damp his ardour … dear God, please don't send him to Rome!

As I was leaving, the abbot shook my hand. 'Explore pleasure for five years,' he suggested, 'then come back here and repent with us.'

'That's not the point,' I thought sulkily. 'That's really not the point at all.'

That afternoon I sat in Port of Spain's Woodford Square eating a vanilla and guava yoghurt. It really hit the spot. Funny how such small pleasures can be so exquisite, isn't it? The Junior Carnival had just ended but the music was still blaring. No, that's not true. If it had been in England you would have described it as blaring; here it was just music. People walking across the park would suddenly start dancing – not showing off, not even dancing with anyone else, but simply doing it for the joy of it. Father John was right. Carnival really is a deeply happy time – a 'bacchanal', as the calypso singers tell us, probably because it's the only word they can think of that has a reasonable stab at rhyming with 'carnival'. But like a lot of pleasure, it's tinged with anxiety. I flipped through the local paper. The big story on page one was about a statement from the Commissioner of Police. It had been rumoured that gangs of ruffians would try to disrupt the festivities, but the army and police 'will use all resources available to us to ensure that your safety is protected'. The letters page was full of complaints about lewd behaviour and racism in the calypso lyrics. Elsewhere there was a cartoon of a little girl in the carnival saying to a policewoman, 'No, Miss … am not lorst … ah jes doh want tuh be seen wit' marmie … she only doin' dose vulgar dances.' It was as though deep down there was a feeling that this amount of liberty and licence was sinful and was bound to lead to divine punishment.

A crowd had gathered on the far side of the square. I ambled over. A tall, middle-aged man was selling ointments and potions. He'd got a deep, booming voice and was dressed from head to toe in baggy red, white and green ceremonial clothes like an African head of state. It was Bushman, the medicine man. Elderly women with pains in their backs sat on a bench while his assistants rubbed the affected area with bright-coloured gunge that smelled like Vick Vapour Rub. An elderly man in the crowd heckled him in defence of the healing qualities of spinach. The women declared they felt much better – but as it looked like it was the first time they'd sat down all day, I wasn't particularly amazed.

Bushman invited me to try some of his potions, and the crowd laughed in anticipation. He had a razor-sharp wit and was obviously an intelligent man – he told us in his spiel that he had been educated at the International College in Togo and had fought in Vietnam. The audience grew bigger. Pretty soon I was brim-full of medicines and unguents. He'd even pushed an anti-congestion remedy up my nostrils and rubbed my Adam's apple with something that cured asthma. After each ministration I declared myself satisfied, and the assistants nodded their approval. Bushman and I had become an improvisational double act. I was undoubtedly the stooge – but what the hell, we were doing great business.

It was at that moment that I committed a faux pas. He'd given me a polystyrene cup full of dark brown sludge. I don't remember what malady it was supposed to address, but I gulped it down manfully. Well, I meant to. I hadn't expected it to throw my throat into a state of complete crisis. I had a flashback to my seventh Christmas when my uncle Stan gave me a sip of his whisky, and everyone fell about laughing as I coughed and spluttered and dedicated myself to a life of total abstinence.

The brown liquid came hurtling back up again, all down my T-shirt, and all down Bushman's red, white and green regalia. Had this been my only mistake, I think I might just about have got away with it. But then he asked me if I'd liked the taste, and I said 'No!' I said it quite forcibly, actually.

There should be a new Bateman cartoon: 'THE MAN WHO TOLD THE MEDICINE MAN HE DIDN'T LIKE HIS MEDICINE'. In an instant, Bushman underwent a complete personality change. Whereas before, he had been avuncular, charming, a real crowd-pleaser – a sort of black Michael Barrymore – he was now the proud, angry, wounded African. Like all white people, I'd come to his country, full of airs and graces, in order to sneer at his medicines. Well, history was changing; I wasn't going to get away with it like Cecil Rhodes and General Gordon had. That medicine tasted just fine, and I knew it. And I'd better tell the crowd how good it was pretty damn quick or suffer the consequences.

Now normally under these circumstances I wilt and stutter, and spray everything and everybody with a thick coating of guilt and apology. For the last twenty years I've lived in Bristol, England. We practically invented the tobacco trade; and the sugar trade; and the rum trade; not to mention the slave trade. I don't have to be told – I'm guilty as hell.

Maybe it was the medicine that did it. After all, I had drunk a good half-bottle of bright pink 'Man's Potion'. Or maybe I was still rather narked that I'd let Louise walk all over me. Whatever the reason, suddenly I wasn't having this guy telling me I'd pretended to spew up his medicine. I really had spewed it up – this was a question of honour.

I started to protest my innocence, but he just shouted louder. So I shouted louder. There we were, in the middle of Woodford Square, yelling at each other nose to chest.

And then he'd gone, and the crowd had gone too. A fresh bunch of punters had gathered round the stall, and Bushman was starting his pitch all over again. I stood there in the middle of the path, all alone, shaking slightly but quite proud of myself. And I'd still got my vanilla and guava yoghurt to finish off.

Three o'clock next morning I woke up and crawled back into town. There were a lot of people around – not really a crowd, more like little wandering clumps of people waiting to become a crowd. I could hear drumming and music some way off, but it was hard to work out precisely which direction they were coming from. I walked for maybe twenty minutes. Was the atmosphere getting tense, or was it just me dressing the moment with a suitable emotion? I was certainly feeling edgy. It'd be sunrise soon and I'd have missed it all. It was like the night the Hackney riots broke out. My friend Gareth from the Flying Pickets and I spent the whole evening looking for insurrection. We wandered from Hackney Marshes to the Balls Pond Road and never found as much as a broken window; then we went home and watched the looting on the telly.

I came to a crossroads. Everyone was looking in the same direction. I pushed my way to the front. What was happening? Nothing. Then suddenly the crowd – it was definitely a crowd now – spun round 180 degrees, and I got my first glimpse of 'J'ouvert', the prelude to the day's big event. Three or four intersections away what looked like a massive wall of speakers was slowly, ever so slowly, crossing the junction blaring samba-like party music, and all round it were the shadowy figures of dancers in weird costumes.

Then I heard more drumming coming from somewhere nearer. Up another side street I caught glimpses of more dancers; then more; and more. The whole town had come alive in little processions of two or three hundred people dancing this way and that in the darkness to the accompaniment of lorryloads of music.

Suddenly, without warning, I was swept up in the dance by a host of revellers who were covered in oil and mud and pink paint. A crazy old Rasta beckoned to me. I danced over to him and in a flash he had my shirt off and was pouring cocoa butter all over me. It was in my hair, my ears, my mouth, dripping down my trousers. I kept on dancing. What else was there to do? The Rasta was yelling. I was yelling too. 'Carnival's even better than a good shit!' he bawled. And I whooped and hollered and fervently agreed with him. Someone put devils' horns on my head; I was in the centre of a group of laughing, hand-clapping fiends from Hell. I was pulled to the ground and lay under a heap of giggling maniacs.

'Call the doctor!' people were shouting. A man dressed in white, holding something that looked like an oversized haggis, lurched over to us. 'This man is dead!' roared the Rasta, 'Make him well again.'

The doctor listened to my heart and thumped various parts of my body. 'He needs the Water of Life!'

'Yeah, the Water of Life!' went the crowd, and he squeezed his haggis. A pee-stream of liquid jetted into my mouth. I swallowed, and when it hit my stomach I knew it wasn't water. It was rum. An awful lot of rum! They heaved me to my feet.

'Are his knees trembling?' demanded the Rasta. They didn't seem to be.

'No!' went the crowd, and suddenly I was on my back again being pumped full of more Water of Life.

'Are his knees trembling now?' went the Rasta. I sure as hell made certain they were. They trembled and shook and shaked and I went bopping down the road, arms swinging, legs kicking, feet tip-tip-tapping, and it wasn't a show and I was totally oblivious to every-one else. I was just dancing my dance in the middle of the carnival.

Suddenly a young woman leaped out of the shadows and gave herself to me. She really did. She had big breasts, and thighs like a baby ox, and she was covered from head to foot in something black and slippery, and she engulfed me in her wonderful bosoms and ground into me with her pelvis like a pestle and mortar, and I was holding on for all I was worth, desperately trying to give as good as I was getting (and I was getting pretty good, believe me), but she was as slidey as an eel, and she was pushing me backwards with those baby-ox thighs and I just hung in there like a prop forward in the seventy-eighth minute. And it went on and on and on, and her friends were laughing and giggling, and I'm thinking, 'Yes, this is rude, of course it's rude, but it's really innocent too. We're not going to fuck, we're just playing, it's only a dance. And we can say and do anything, and there'll be no heartache, no recriminations. This is Bacchanal! This is what Bacchanal really is!'

I got back to the hotel about 10.30 a.m., to grab some rest before the main carnival in the afternoon. The air conditioning sounded like a tractor being driven up a muddy hill, there was a dog fight in the courtyard, and Byron Lee and his Dragonnaires were testing their lorryload of amplification systems in the car park. 'One!' went the roadie. 'One One! One Two! One!' I got to 874 and fell asleep.

*Pages 85-91: Spectacular outfits, ear-splitting music and plenty
of 'Water of Life' make Carnival an unforgettable experience.*

*Previous page, above: Tony (in borrowed Devil's horns) and friend
at 'J'ouvert', the overture to Carnival proper, in the early hours of
Monday morning in Port of Spain.*

*Previous page, below: Decoratively smeared in oil, cocoa butter
and pink paint, a Trinidadian sets out for the serious business
of Carnival.*

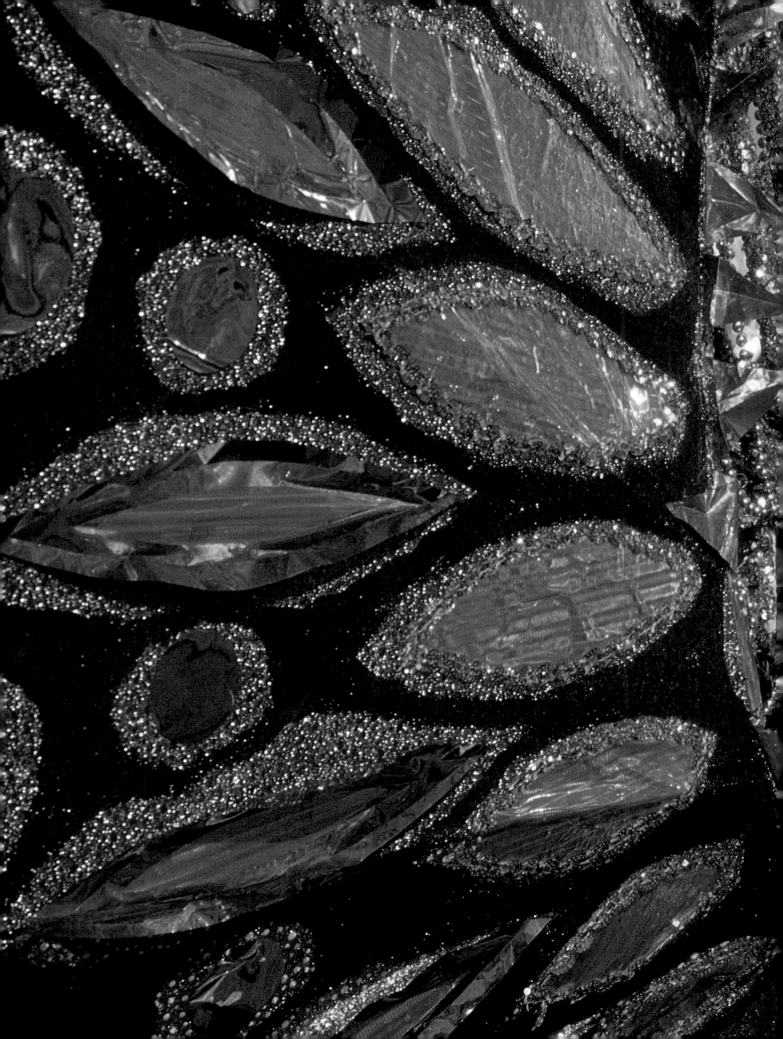

What can I tell you about Carnival? It was spectacular, colourful, no one tried to mug me, or pick my pocket, or sell me drugs. Everyone was very friendly. But – and it's a But the size of a pregnant water buffalo – have you ever spent the entire day at a carnival? The first hour's fine: you're showing off your flashy costume, you're part of a group of happy-go-lucky revellers, there's a jolly kind of mindless solidarity in the air. Then you notice your shoulder straps are chafing you under the armpits, and the ties round your legs are working loose, and the Velcro starts to lose its grip, and so do you. When the procession grinds to a halt, you're pretty relieved. You can do a few running repairs, straighten out your sequins etcetera. But an hour goes by, then two, and you're stuck in exactly the same place, and the heat's getting to you, and you're wedged six inches from a bank of speakers that've been blasting the same calypso at you all morning, and you want a pee, and you're dying for a drink but your stupid costume's so skimpy there was nowhere to put your wallet....

By mid-afternoon, tripping slightly from mild sunstroke, I'd jacked it in. I dodged through ranks of amateur video-makers, past the roti sellers, and the curried goat vendors, and staggered back to the hotel. It looked much more spectacular on the TV – and I could go to the lav whenever I wanted.

I wouldn't have missed it, of course. It was a once-in-a-lifetime experience and every-thing. But it was only a show. It wasn't real. The designs weren't the quirky expression of individual imaginations. Carnival's big business now. The top ten West Indian designers fly back from the opera houses of Europe each year to sketch stunning concepts which are turned out by the thousand and sold to Trinidadians for 600 dollars a time. And the steel bands have almost disappeared, drowned beneath waves of amplified calypso and soca.

There was a time when Carnival was real; when for two days of the year the blighted people of this blighted island could forget their poverty and humiliation and become wild, furious, drum-banging demons. But those days are long gone. Well, not quite. There's still J'ouvert. That was real. Really real. It was good to be alive that morning.

Dominica

I chartered a tiny six-seater to Dominica. I couldn't get there on a scheduled flight because Dominica doesn't have an international airport. For that matter it doesn't have a TV station, or a railway network, or shower gel, or wheel clamps. It does have traffic lights, but only one set.

This is Bounty Bar country, every white man's fantasy of what a tropical paradise should really be like. 'Untouched', 'Unspoiled', the vocabulary of the holiday brochure sounds a little less jaded than usual when you're in Dominica.

To explore it properly, I knew I needed to tread softly, to be at one with Nature, to blur into the landscape like an Indian hunter. Well, that was my original intention. But then I saw this 600cc Honda for hire. It was red, mean and made a noise like the soundtrack of Apocalypse Now. Ecologically it was pretty unsound, but I loved it from the moment it coughed and spluttered into life like a bad-tempered miner at a silicosis medical.

92

In Jamaica and Trinidad every day had been clearly defined – Dance Hall happened on Wednesday, Carnival on a Tuesday. But my impressions of Dominica are a timeless, jumbled sprawl. Tropical rainforests, amazing sunsets, deep green banana plantations, fast-flowing crystal-clear rivers – I sped by them and past them and through them in a dramatic reverie. I was the last of the great sixties' bikers and I was living dangerously – in Dominica they don't have crash helmets either.

One episode does stand out though: the mountain chicken hunt. I'd never even heard of mountain chickens, but Elkin told me you could catch them in the dead of night down by the river after a heavy rainfall. You had to move fast though, 'cos once the little blighters got into a blue funk, they'd hop, jump and swim like bats out of hell.

Elkin was Miss Henry's father. She ran the bar in Main Street, and each night he'd hold court there, a scruffy, bleary-eyed old man with the accent and manners of an Old Etonian. The bar was tumbledown and rudimentary, with a solitary light bulb illuminating a hand-written sign saying: 'TONIGHT'S SPECIAL – BLACK PUDDING AND GOAT WATER'. But above the blare of the soul music (Fontella Bass singing 'Rescue Me' on a tape so old and slow that she sounded like Louis Armstrong) you could hear Elkin's plummy tone sounding off about medieval English history, the Irish Question, international labour law, but most of all about the comparative qualities of his collection of rums. There must have been thirty bottles on the bar – Cocksure Rum, Rosemary Rum, and the king of all rums, Bois Bondé, white soca rum infused with the bark of the Bois Bondé tree that was so potent it stiffened you up, straightened you out and got you lovemaking ten times a night without once having to feign a headache. And as, according to Miss Henry, Elkin had sired twenty-three children, I wasn't inclined to disbelieve him.

Eventually my two co-hunters, Alexis and his father McDonald, arrived. They dragged me out into the night, handed me a bottle of kerosene with a Kleenex tissue jammed into its neck for a wick, and off we set for the mountain chicken hunt.

We waited by the river for a long time. It was pitch-black except for our kerosene torches and a flickering Tilley lamp that looked in dire need of some Bois Bondé. Alexis was whispering, telling me about the various large animals that lived in these parts. Except his words were half patois, half English, and I couldn't understand what animals he was talking about. That is until he said the word 'boa constrictor'. Even in the hopelessly inadequate torchlight, he must have noticed how pale I'd gone. 'S'OK,' he said. 'D'ere no poison snakes – dey jez bite a little.' I think he was trying to reassure me. He didn't succeed. I felt like someone who'd been handed a smoking bomb with the words 'Ozone friendly' on it. McDonald hadn't said anything all evening, and he didn't now. He just cackled a lot, then burst into fits of coughing.

The rum was churning in my guts. I wanted to go home. I wanted to find BBC World Service on my radio. I wanted to rub calamine on my sunburn. I wanted to do anything except be in this alien forest surrounded by snakes, unspecified wild animals and a mad old man.

Along with sugar cane, pineapples, spices and coffee, bananas are
an important crop for many Caribbean islands. So far the banana
plantations of Dominica have kept the island mercifully free of
tourism, but it may not stay that way much longer.

Opposite: A boat on Indian River, which flows through mangrove
swamps and a rainforest in the north of island.

*A colourful shop front in the village of St Joseph on the west coast
of the island of Dominica.*

Opposite: A child playing in the street in St Joseph.

*Overleaf: Lush vegetation surrounds houses on a steep hillside
near St Joseph.*

Suddenly McDonald let out a little yelp, then shot off, leaping crazily from rock to rock. There was a tiny splash, and he was in the river. He grabbed at something, missed it, then grabbed it again. He came wading out of the water, eyes shining with triumph, holding a small, struggling something in his hands. It was bleating like a cross between a bird and a sheep.

'Mountain chicken!' he crowed victoriously, and thrust it into my hands.

It was a frog. Not a sweet little itsy-bitsy frog like the ones you dissect in the biology lab. This one must have weighed in at about one and a half pounds. I stared at it stupidly, and it stared straight back. It looked like a small, haughty human. No wonder there are all those stories about princes being turned into frogs. And no wonder the princesses found it such an ordeal trying to snog them. My one would have had your tongue off in five seconds flat.

Next day I ate it. Alexis lives on the other side of Main Street in a tiny two-room house so clean you could eat your frogs off the linoleum. He'd marinaded mine overnight in peppers, onion and spices, then fried it in breadcrumbs. You'll notice I refer to my frog prince as 'it'. Actually I'd christened him Graham, and lunch felt a bit cannibalistic.

I remembered a story I'd heard about the Carib Indians. They loved Europeans. They loved them so much they'd slice open their backs, stuff their wounds with herbs and pimentos, then kill them, cook them and eat them. The French were considered the tastiest, followed by the Dutch and the English. But apparently the Spanish were a culinary disaster − stringy, gristly, and with a slightly bitter aftertaste − unlike Graham, who was exquisite. And yes, he did taste like chicken.

Until I came to Dominica, I'd thought Columbus and his men had wiped the Caribs off the face of the earth. I was wrong. Alexis took me to the Carib reservation − a few square miles of rugged mountains and inhospitable coastline where the last two thousand surviving West Indian Indians make a rudimentary living.

Julius Corriette is a well-travelled, middle-aged Carib, who wears a peaked cap saying 'Royal Canadian Mounted Police'. Tens of thousands of years ago, he told me, at the time when all the continents joined together, the Caribs had lived in China. They'd slowly made their way down to South America until, maybe six thousand years ago, they'd sailed to the mouth of the Orinoco and then across the mighty ocean to the West Indies. And, no, they weren't cannibals. That was a lie − black propaganda put out by the Europeans to justify their policy of genocide. Sure, the Caribs used to keep the heads of their defeated enemies in their huts. But that was because they liked to have decorative trophies around the house, just like Victorian gentlemen kept the heads of rhinoceros and elephants hanging in their billiard rooms.

It was ironic, he said. The only reason Columbus was able to set sail was because the Europeans liked their food so much. Constantinople had fallen to the Turks, the spice route from the Far East had closed, and suddenly the groaning tables of France, Spain and Merrie England were short of nutmeg and cloves and cinnamon. That's why the Spanish court had subsidized Columbus – to find a new spice route. And in discovering Dominica (on a Sunday, hence the name) he'd initiated five centuries of misery and exploitation.

And the Caribs had welcomed their tormentors with open arms. They were a proud, free, unencumbered people. If the Europeans wanted their gold, it was only courteous to give it to them. And in return, the Europeans gave them little bells that rang prettily, and that was a fair exchange. Except that next time the Europeans landed they had soldiers with them, and they told the Caribs to fill their little bells with gold dust and hand them over; because if they didn't they'd have their arms cut off. So now there was a new exchange. In return for the bell full of gold, each Carib was given a little metal tag to hang round his neck, so that if he met a European he wouldn't be dismembered.

And then the fighting began, and whole tribes of Caribs were slaughtered. And other armies arrived, and they brought with them black men and women in chains; slaves from Mali, Dahomey and the Congo. But sometimes the slaves ran away into the hills and joined the Caribs as guerrilla fighters. And century followed bloody century, and now all the Caribs were dead. All except the few in this tiny piece of Dominica that's so mountainous their enemies never quite managed to flush them out.

And the Europeans are still here too, of course, only they aren't soldiers any more. They're representatives from international corporations telling the Dominicans to grow more bananas. A lot more bananas. And even more. So that the whole landscape has become dominated by banana plantations. That's why it's remained such a beautiful island. The Dominicans have never been given the chance to build anything – just told to pick fruit off the trees. Only now the international corporations are telling them they won't buy their bananas any longer. On the other side of the world, a treaty called GATT has been signed, which means the bananas from Costa Rica and the Philippines will be cheaper than those from Dominica. They won't be as big, of course, or as sweet. But will the people of Bruges and Memphis and Westbury-on-Trym care about that? So the Dominicans will have to find another way to survive. Tourism? Yes, there'll undoubtedly be tourism. Nature trails will be blazed through the rainforest. There'll be cafeterias, litter bins, advertising hoardings. And, I don't doubt, nightclubs, prostitutes, crack, venereal disease. It's a fair exchange, and the Caribs know all about fair exchange. Dominica has given us the perfect picture of a tropical paradise; the least we can do in return is offer it our late twentieth-century pleasure industry.

Dominican Republic

It's a thousand miles from Dominica, but their names are pretty similar. I'm sorry about that, but there's very little I could do about it – except maybe go to Guadaloupe instead.

The Dominican Republic is half of the old pirate island of Hispaniola, the other half being Haiti. On the way there, I asked our Finnish pilot if the Republic was as crazy a place as I'd heard. The impression I had was that it would be a bit like a Latin American version of the Wild West.

'No, that's not fair,' said the pilot fervently. 'Sure, people carry guns, but they don't shoot anyone. Maybe they'll do a little armed robbery now and then, but they're not bad people.'

'So why do they carry guns?'

'It's a macho thing. They used to have this dictator, Trujillo, a really bad guy. You needed guns then, and the habit kinda stuck.'

'So is it a corrupt place?'

'No! Well, maybe, yes. If you want things done, you usually have to spend a little.'

'What kind of things?'

'Well, like with the plane. Hold on! I've got to negotiate with air traffic control – see if they'll let us touch down.'

I had no idea how I'd react to a cockfight, but one thing I wasn't expecting was such a pretty cockpit. It was circular, made of wood and painted strawberry ice-cream pink, like a bandstand on the prom at Folkestone. And inside, it was clean and tidy with four concentric circles of seats (green, blue, red and pink) round an artificial grass stage. Were there a few slightly darker patches on the grass? Maybe it was just the dappled light.

This was a cockpit to be proud of, and Felicia, the owner's wife, certainly was. She was a Puerto Rican New Yorker, and still worked in the Big Apple six months of the year as a nutritionist on an aid programme for disadvantaged mothers and children. But the rest of the year she based herself in the Dominican Republic, drawing up plans for a cockpit mark II, with catering facilities, a bigger car park and new bathrooms, 'so the guys don't make a mess all over the place.'

It was two o'clock in the afternoon in the middle of a torrential tropical storm. The spectators, all men, were crowded round the bar and the weighing rooms, arguing furiously in that Latin way that seems to require your whole body. Four young musicians were wiring up their amplifiers while their assistant tested the mikes. *'Uno!'* he went. *'Uno! Dos! Uno! Dos!'* The oral poetry of roadies the world over. The only women in sight were two adolescent girls chewing gum, their mini-skirts tight round their bums like clingfilm round a lamb's kidney.

For the owners, the spectators and particularly for the birds, the preparations were deadly serious. There were a hundred little rituals, a hundred tiny adjustments. The cocks were weighed, matched against suitable opponents, their bellies shaved, suitable spurs chosen and then taped slowly and scrupulously to their ankles – or at least to the place their ankles would have been if birds had ankles. And every procedure was conducted at full volume, with brothers, cousins, friends and hecklers jostling for prime position in order to offer their own special piece of advice.

The rain hammered down on the corrugated iron roof. Water swirled round the feet of the tiny shoeshine boys scrubbing away at dusty plastic shoes whose owners were oblivious to everything except the fury with which they were currently making their point.

With a howl of feedback, the band started to play a merengue, that slow, sultry rhythm that sounds so sexy in a Latin country, and so pathetically plinky-plonky when you play it back home. Time dragged endlessly on. It was 3.45 p.m. now. When would the fighting start? I was half-bored, half-fascinated and a tad claustrophobic. Then suddenly the rain stopped, the sun came out and everyone began to drift towards the bandstand.

A policeman checked for guns at the entrance, then, like a hat-check girl, glued a cloakroom ticket to each one and put it in a small, white cupboard that reminded me of my bathroom cabinet. I felt slightly embarrassed when my shirt buttons got caught up with the butt of someone's pistol, but we had a little laugh about it and everything was all right again.

Inside, two assistants dressed in white coats were holding the first two fighting cocks at arm's length while the judge wound up a huge, old-fashioned timepiece that looked like the front of a grandfather clock. A third bird was carried into the ring and shaken tantalizingly close to the fighters, who grew more and more frustrated as they tried to claw its head off.

The second hand was turned to twelve. For a moment, the din subsided. The fighting birds were placed on the ground. There was a second's pause, then they flew at each other. A roar erupted that made everything before it seem mere chatter.

The main thing I remember is how small the birds were, and how totally passionate the crowd was. There's a quality of size about Riddick and Holyfield and Tyson that make the spectators' reaction somehow appropriate, but these chickens were the size of an egg box. You could have stepped on one and put it out of its misery. Yet they seemed to summon up the Furies in the soul of every man in the crowd – two hundred Orestes totally consumed by blood-lust.

Peck! Peck! Peck! Peck! Tiny eyes were jabbed out, little spinal cords were severed, beaks were ripped off, torn cockscombs lay quivering on the astroturf.

Fight followed fight followed fight. Unbelievably, passions grew even hotter. In mid-bout, a spectator stormed across the circle to gesticulate and bawl at someone opposite. Everyone near joined in, while those behind yelled at them to sit down. A crazed chicken, its head little more than a bloody, featureless stump, ran round and round the ring pursued by its assailant, while the crowd jeered and catcalled at its cowardice.

I had blood on my legs and specks of blood on my glasses. I staggered outside exhausted, my head thumping.

And yet.... ! There was a kind of pleasure in it. A deep, dark, guilty pleasure maybe, like the seamy fantasy that sneaks into your mind late at night in a lonely hotel room. But a pleasure nevertheless.

I've felt something similar at soccer matches. I remember watching Tottenham Hotspur versus Wimbledon on the telly, and seeing John Fashanu ram his elbow into Gary Mabbutt's face. Seventeen stitches Mabbutt got and he was out for the rest of the season. The papers said it was a disgrace and it probably was, but we all watched the action replay

103

Passions are easily aroused at cockfights, so a policeman checks
the arriving audience for weapons. Each gun is assigned a numbered
cloakroom ticket and placed in a cupboard to be collected later.

Opposite: A 'sport' that's cruel and violent,
which usually ends in death or hideous mutilation.

and studied the photos and talked about it for weeks afterwards, and it was ever so exciting, and I know if I'd been a Wimbledon supporter, a part of me would have been whispering 'Go on, Fash! Go on, my son! You get stuck in.'

Because if pain's an evolutionary signal telling us what to avoid, maybe pleasure's nature's way of telling us what we need. Sweet things are good because they give us energy, friendly people are good because they afford us protection, and blood and passion are good because they encourage us to defend ourselves. Whether these deep signals which were so handy on the prehistoric African savannah are as appropriate in present-day Santo Domingo or Basildon, is another matter.

But next time I go to the Spurs, next time I walk through the entrance to White Hart Lane, look up and see their boldly emblazoned emblem, the fighting cock, at least I'll know a bit more about the spectacle I'm taking part in.

I'd heard that the beach at Boca Chica was chock-full of young Dominican girls on the look-out for European husbands, and hordes of randy, middle-aged German men who come over on special tourist packages each year for a bit of fun and frolic, only to be permanently ensnared by the wiles of the Dominican *chicas*. Speedy marriages, said an advert in the local paper, cost 100 US dollars, speedy divorces, 500 dollars.

So did the beach live up to its advance publicity? Yes. My expectations were confirmed, reconfirmed, then stamped with a big rubber stamp saying: 'THESE EXPECTA-TIONS HAVE BEEN SUPERSEDED BY REALITY'.

Things started quite slowly. It was a family beach – lots of little children, vendors selling inflatable frogs, that sort of thing. Certainly there were a few dusky maidens sitting on the sand with men of a lighter hue, but they could well have been nice girls out of Chicago or Detroit talking to their fiancés about the postcard list.

I wandered into a beachside café. Two little boys were strumming tunelessly on home-made banjos and singing 'Quantanamera'. I paid them to leave. An old man with an accordion approached. 'Quantanamera' again. Then someone put on a merengue CD, and out of a back room sashayed three young girls dressed in what looked like tiny black string shopping bags. They had bright red lips and demanding, playful eyes that checked out everyone in the café. Each one looked like she was the sexiest girl in the world and she knew it. Two more young girls came in – they can't have been more than fourteen years old – then a few more, till there were maybe a dozen of them, all behaving like they owned the place, brazenly approaching complete strangers, ruffling their hair, drinking their drinks, touching their faces. It was extraordinary. It might have seemed appropriate in a sleazy nightclub around two in the morning, but this was a family beach at lunchtime. I really wanted to hear what they were saying to the men they were chatting up, but I was being accosted by a magician with a Mohican haircut who had a cigarette in his ear and was blowing the smoke out his mouth. At any other time I'd have been impressed, but now I was just irritated.

I went down to the water's edge and lay on a sunbed. Two pretty young men with bleached hair were in deep, meaningful conversation with a large-breasted German *Frau*. 'Santipankis' – that's what they were, the Dominican name for gigolos. I wondered where the word had come from. Could it be a corruption of 'hanky-panky'? Hanky-panky! What an absurd euphemism. No Dominican could have invented a word like that. It must have been a Brit.

My reverie was broken by a bony pelvis landing somewhere below my belly button. 'Massage?' asked the owner of the pelvis. 'Good massage?' There have been moments in my life when mind and spirit have been so confused, so paralyzed by the pitched battle between guilt and curiosity, that my body has been forced to take over the steering wheel. This was just such a moment. My internal movie screen threw up a confusion of images from *Fatal Attraction* and various AIDS documentaries, not to mention a few stills of my beautiful, trusting girlfriend back home, but my body nodded its head. Immediately, my masseuse let out a mischievous little chuckle, did a few thrusting movements with her pelvis and plunged her fingers into my chest hair, like a kitten into the best sofa.

Her name was Maria and I've never been sat on by anyone perter. She had a pert nose, pert breasts, pert teeth, pert chin – she was also extremely lazy. After she'd been pummelling away for about ninety seconds flat, she pulled a face like someone who'd had a tiring day at the office and then discovered the car stereo's been nicked. '*Ay! Soy cansada!*' she said, and called imperiously to her friend Consuela, who was chubby, with bad teeth. Consuela was consigned to my lower regions. There was lots of toe wiggling and nipple pulling. The two girls invented this game whereby Consuela would suddenly lift my legs up 90 degrees, which would send Maria tumbling into my face. We all thought this was pretty amusing, although I began to get the impression that my participation wasn't particularly important – in fact, even though it was supposed to be my body that was being worked on, I felt rather ignored. In halting, failed O-Level Spanish, I managed to evince the fact that Maria was twenty-one, although I wasn't sure I believed her: she didn't look a day older than my seventeen-year-old daughter. No, we'll forget that comparison, thank you. How would I feel if Laura went on the game? God! I'd rather she joined the Moonies or married Michael Portillo.

Maria also told me she was unhappy here and wanted to come with me to Europe. Either that or she was happy here and didn't want to come with me to Europe, I wasn't sure which. She had a few stabs at the sentence, then became distracted by Consuela who'd left my feet in order to plait some large, garish plastic beads into my fringe, and was now whacking my nose with them like a kid playing conkers.

Was this pleasure? What would the lads in the pub think when I told them I'd been massaged by two young prostitutes on a Caribbean beach? The truth was, it was about as much fun as baby-sitting a couple of hyperactive nine-year-olds.

Then a voice in my ear said, '*Otra naranja, señor?*' It was the waiter with another drink, his face as discreet and detached as the receptionist at a clap clinic. I fumbled in my shorts,

107

*On the beach at Boca Chica, everyone seems to be offering
or looking for sex.*

*Opposite: Among other services available on the sands is
hair-braiding.*

drew out a wad of notes, peeled a couple off and gave them to him. With a cry of triumph Maria snatched the rest in payment, and she and Consuela ran laughing and giggling along the water's edge into the distance.

I grabbed for my glasses, but was slightly hampered by the baby oil I'd been drenched in, and by the forest of beads which kept banging into my eyes. By the time I could see again the girls were fifty yards away, chatting up a couple of muscular young hippies. I felt abandoned and ripped off. I'd been worked over as efficiently as I would have been by a couple of stallholders in the Ridley Road Market.

I don't think I liked Maria very much, but I certainly admired her. I find it hard to imagine her ending up in Düsseldorf married to a plastic garden furniture representative. But then she probably won't, will she? I doubt if she'd have the patience … or the concentration.

The one thing my Dad feared above all else was going 'gaga'. I can vividly remember the look of loathing and contempt on his face when he said the word. Why did this particular state upset him so much? I don't know. Maybe he somehow knew that Altzheimer's Syndrome lay waiting to grace the last year of his life. I never really knew what 'gaga' meant, but I could tell you how it felt. It was the noise babies made. It was mindless and incoherent and humiliating … and it was very frightening.

So when I was invited to a 'gaga' ceremony, it was these emotions that started churning around inside me. 'Gaga', I was told, is Dominican for 'voodoo', and somewhere on the border between the Dominican Republic and Haiti I was going to witness a community of Haitian refugees performing one of their dark, pre-Easter gaga ceremonies.

I'd always assumed that voodoo was a primitive cult, practised only by the poor and the spiritually confused, but my guide and mentor couldn't have been less primitive. Jean-Michel Caroit is the Caribbean correspondent for *Le Monde*. He's like a character out of a novel by Sartre – witty, artistic, widely read, politically sophisticated, brave (he's one of that tiny band of journalists who continually risk capture and torture by sneaking over the border into Haiti), and he's got an absurd Inspector Clouseau accent and a haughty Gallic shrug. He also believes in voodoo.

He took me for a walk through a street market in Santo Domingo. The market stalls were piled high with brightly coloured fruit, veg and battery-operated consumer products. I found it hard to believe that the Dominican Republic is one of the poorest countries in the Caribbean. I associate poverty with mud huts and barren smallholdings, not drum-banging rabbits. Then Jean-Michel pointed out a row of open-fronted shops half-hidden behind the stalls. At first glance they appeared to be selling hairspray and deodorants, but closer inspection revealed that the various bottles and aerosols bore pictures of Catholic saints on their labels.

'All-Purpose Spray,' announced one. 'It's Dominating, Conquering, gives you Fast Luck, Protection, Divine Eye, Money Driving and Peace. 33% Free. Do not Puncture or

Incinerate.' Clearly the great gods Market Forces and Free Enterprise were at work even here in Santo Domingo. The world of the spirit had been packaged, put into a CFC-free spray can and sold at a knock-down price.

The drive to the border that evening was long and arduous. The A-road became a B-road which in turn became a muddy track. After an hour or so of bumps and potholes, a shadowy figure loomed into the headlights. This was the young initiate, dressed in an ancient Van Halen T-shirt and New York Giants cap, who was going to lead us to the night's events.

In the West any ceremony, whether it's a play, a court case or the Lord Mayor's parade, has a beginning, a middle and an end. One minute you're in the real world, then the show starts and, until it finishes, you inhabit its coded universe of symbols and funny costumes. But that's not how things work in the Caribbean. I didn't realize the ceremony was underway for ages. People were laughing and giggling, Honda 50s were weaving in and out of the crowd, rum was being passed round and consumed at an alarming rate. Sure, there was singing, but maybe this was just the warm-up, because if this was the actual voodoo, why were there so many little children still up? I'd heard that these events could go on till daybreak. Surely they'd have to break off and put the kids to bed?

Then an old woman started to quiver and shake; her head was lolling and the crowd was urging her on excitedly. But was she really going gaga? She still had her arm round a young boy – her grandson, I suppose. He seemed completely unconcerned. Occasionally he'd look up and smile at her and, in mid-quake, she'd smile back. Jean-Michel whispered to me that, at some time during the night, a ghostly horse and rider would take possession of one of the worshippers. Many would begin to feel his influence, but only one would be chosen. And no one would know who that was until the moment arrived.

So what kind of religion is it that encourages you to worship and get legless at the same time? I asked. The voodoo gods aren't respectable like our own Trinity, Jean-Michel explained; they're deeply sensual, pleasure-loving deities, created out of the union between the old animistic African gods and the Catholic pantheon of saints. They have urges that need satisfying, and recognize that their congregation do too. In gaga, rewards aren't deferred till some later date in Heaven. If you want a new lover, slender hips or a stye removed from your eye, you simply ask the gods, and, provided you get the formula right, your wish is granted.

I couldn't see much evidence of wish fulfilment. The village had no electric light, no running water, no sewers. The ceremony was taking place round the back of the communal privies and the smell was awful.

The villagers danced on and on. It was three o'clock in the morning now and everyone seemed to be having far too good a time to stop. Maybe taking part was more important to them than their dreams coming true. I knew I hadn't the energy to stay to the end. I had to fly back to England in a few hours. There were suitcases to pack, customs officers to appease, not to mention a nine-hour stopover in Caracas. I drove back thinking

that gaga wasn't for me. It's a religion for a hot country. I'm from the northern tribes. We live in the cold, we're fearful of winter, and deep in our genes is an overwhelming need to plan ahead and avoid starvation. Caution, not wild abandon, runs through our Anglo-Saxon veins. We're too mistrustful to believe we'll be given what we want, or that we deserve to get it.

And so it is with pleasure. Despite the fact that I've seen how easy it is to become immersed in it, deep down I'll go on believing that pleasure's something to which I'm not really entitled, and which I shouldn't really seek. But if I'm very good, it may sneak up unbidden and take me by surprise while I'm doing something useful and sensible, like putting the opened pack of cheese in a plastic bag.

Still, the last three weeks did loosen me up a bit, and that can't be bad. And I have to admit – I did have a really nice time.

Haitian refugees perform a voodoo or 'gaga' ceremony
somewhere on the border between Haiti and the
Dominican Republic.

KOREA
Evelyn Glennie

Translation is a technical skill; interpretation is an art form.

GREG MALCANGI

My desire to become a David Attenborough of percussion, interpreting both familiar and little-known instruments from every continent to musical audiences of all ages, has developed at a rate for which I am immensely thankful. The startling musical discoveries which I have made have helped me to explore what it means to be a musician, and indeed what it means to be me.

One thing which I find intriguing and greatly satisfying in the world of percussion is that there are no class barriers – some of the greatest musicians are amateurs who spend a lifetime specializing in a very narrow area of percussion playing, such as bodhran, marimba, tabla, snaredrum or bones. They aim to become 'one' with their instrument, and to find that crucial internal vibration which transfers them to a level or world which I cannot find words to explain. Commercialism is not normally a temptation, and they guard their knowledge and discoveries fiercely. On my travels, it has been vital to speak the same raw musical language as my new musical friends (if you can't talk, you can't play), for they will only part with knowledge once they realize you are one of them.

In music I soon realized that facts and figures gained from books mean nothing at all – it's when you put them all together that it becomes knowledge. But the spirit, heart,

Village life between Kyongju and Namwon.

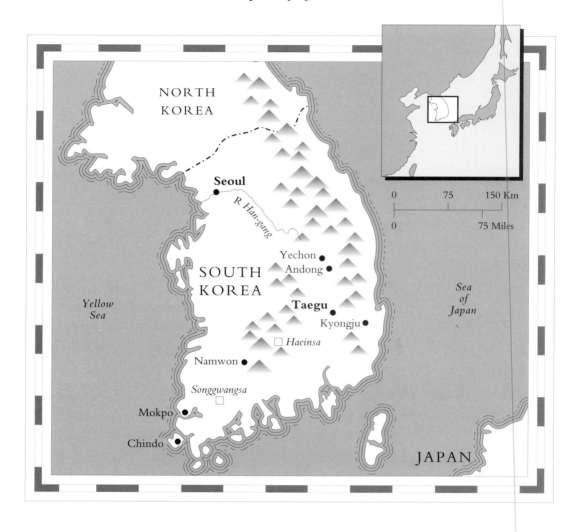

vibration and the unexplainable is born or awakened when you plunge at last into the musical pool.

A journey through the depths of Korea's musical culture, in particular to explore its percussion playing, was an intriguing proposition. At the outset my knowledge of Korean music was limited, and the country was one which I had given little thought to visiting. I required real support in gathering necessary knowledge together and I was extremely grateful and relieved for the research which my colleague, Judy Chesterman, did. But I am like a child – I am curious. I want to broaden my knowledge, discover new sounds and new experiences, and of course expand my ever-increasing range of instruments.

On my travels as a concert performer, I would often like to share new experiences with someone close, but I cannot because it tends to be a lonely life. But in compensation, my solitude and privacy give the surroundings an aura of power, and nothing I see is taken for granted or passed by. Korea was no exception. My thirteen-hour flight from Frankfurt to Seoul was just another time warp with no escape – something which I cannot fight but must simply accept. But I recall with pleasure the view from the plane windows of the expanse below, especially when flying over Siberia. The carved, angular shapes of the land, the desertedness and isolation, are hammered home by knowing that, although much time has passed, down below it is meaningless as there appears to be no civilization. When I peered down, my head filled with sounds and phrases which reflected what I saw. In some ways I so desperately wanted to engulf the whole land and let it know that someone cared for it and loved it! Rather childish, perhaps, but I fantasize....

My touchdown at Seoul and the escape from Kimpo International Airport was an ever-familiar routine, and then I was on the airport shuttle en route to my accommodation in yet another big, impersonal hotel – I would have preferred a *yogwan* (a traditional Korean inn) so that I could have learned more about the country and its culture. On the huge modern roads alongside the sprawl of the River Han-gang I was quickly engulfed in the noise, pollution and traffic chaos of any large Western city. The vast, sprawling conurbation which is home to nearly ten million people began to unfold before my eyes. Having experienced the cultural vibrancy of Japanese cities, of Hong Kong and Taipei, I was, I suppose, expecting a similar sensation from Seoul. But no. The 1988 Olympic city displays the results of a nationwide commitment to industrialization and the achievements of a highly educated, highly motivated workforce. There were skyscrapers galore, most not more than thirty years old, with only a few remaining traditional buildings. Korean culture seemed to be buried beneath the surface of Western influence. I started to feel despondent, for I was looking for ancient tradition to feed my hungry eyes.

My first priority, then, was to wander around Seoul on foot, partly to get a feel for my surroundings but also to capture the secret of Korea's cultural soul. It wasn't easy. Crossing roads was virtually impossible – the dense flow of fast-moving traffic seemed to approach from all directions, and the rules of the road are impossible for a stranger to understand; but fortunately the city is well provided with underpasses. I also required some agility and for-bearance while walking along the streets, for people seemed to be in a hurry and I got bumped and jolted from all directions if I failed to go with the flow. Yet despite the crowds I felt safe – a rare feeling in any city. Seoul's population has mushroomed by some 80 per cent over the past fifteen years or so, partly through a rising birth rate and partly as a result of heavy migration from the countryside. With almost a quarter of all South Koreans living in the capital, it provides an incredible example of how fast things happen and how successful the country has been in its pursuit of rapid economic development.

I found it difficult to know when I was at the heart of Downtown Seoul, since turning a corner from the area of smart hotels brought me into a maze of run-down side streets where I quickly got lost, especially since they have no signboards. Modern Seoul rose from the ashes of the Korean War, which ended in 1953: Korea remains divided between the Communist North and the capitalist South. Many of the buildings I passed, with a few exceptions such as the National Museum, City Hall, Myong-dong cathedral, the Anglican cathedral and the railway, have been built since that time. But my track also led me to the Namdaemun Gate, which was originally built in 1398 as part of a wall to fortify the newly proclaimed capital. It is now known as the Great South Gate, although its signboard calls it

The Namdaemun Gate dates from 1398, when it was built as part of a fortified wall surrounding medieval Seoul. Designated National Treasure No. 1 by the present regime, it now stands incongruously juxtaposed with twentieth-century tower blocks.

Opposite: Night-time Seoul, like most modern cities, is alive with neon signs.

'Sungnyemun' – the Gate of Exalted Ceremony – which I find much more evocative. In the Korean government's praiseworthy attempt to preserve what remains of the country's ancient monuments, Namdaemun is designated as National Treasure No. 1.

Anxious to escape from the concrete surroundings and dense pollution, I wandered across to the landscaped river banks, full of parks and sports fields. The place was beautiful if somewhat crowded, but my eyes were drawn to something I wasn't expecting – live Western-style pop music was being played on a nearby pier, to the accompaniment of distorting cassette recorders!

Down by the river, I decided I could not resist taking a boat cruise. The boats that ply the Han-gang are bright and spacious with upper and lower decks, both enclosed and open, giving a clear view in all directions. My cruise ran for 9 miles, from Yoido to Chamshil. At first there was little of interest, apart from the immensely tall DLI63 building on the south bank, which had been the tallest in Asia when it was built. However, as we passed the centre of Seoul on the north bank it became much more interesting and I wished that this had been my first sight of the city, with the mountain backdrop and Seoul Tower rising 500 feet (152 metres) from the summit of Mount Namsan, which is in the middle of town. I disembarked close to the Seoul sports complex and considered going to the Korean Traditional Performing Arts Centre. But then I decided that I had not come to find carefully preserved court music from a bygone era – 'dead' music which is only performed on ceremonial occasions. What I wanted was to search for 'living' music that was still part of the daily existence of the people. So I returned to the city centre, going over in my mind what I knew about Korean music.

Inevitably my thoughts went first to the Korean musicians I know – the great violinist Kyung Wha Chung and her talented family, who all play Western music. I stood in Korea's Western-style capital and considered the pop music I had heard, and wondered if the truth is that Korea's living music is Western. I knew that the people had suffered badly under Japanese rule from 1910 to 1945, when the foreign regime had tried to suppress the country's history and culture – perhaps it had succeeded.

My subsequent visit to a specialist arts school seemed to confirm my fears. At the Yewon Middle School, where nine hundred twelve- to fifteen-year-olds study music, fine arts or dance in addition to the normal curriculum, I was astounded at the high standard of playing from the musicians. But it was all on Western instruments, and the dancers were studying classical ballet. The Principal mentioned in passing, however, that some of the dancers could study traditional dance if they so wished, and that pupils could go on to learn traditional instruments at university level at the National Music Institute. I began to sense that there was a revival of interest in Korea's own music, but still wondered if it was living and evolving or merely preserved in aspic.

I had read about some musicians called Samul Nori (Samul meaning 'people' and Nori meaning 'play'), whose music had become so popular that there are now several other groups of the same name. So I decided to go and see the original group at NanJang, their

*Music occupies an important place in the Korean school
curriculum, but, as with Yewon Middle School orchestra,
the emphasis is frequently on Western culture.*

rehearsal room in the suburbs of Seoul. Here I met their founder, Kim Duk Soo, and his American assistant, Suzanna Samstag, who explained that their music is based on that of the bands which used to play in every farming village. Each region had different variations in its music and rhythms, but the basic idea was the same. The band would follow the sacred village spirit pole (a flagpole blessed at the local shrine by the shaman or high priest) as the farmers in the social group, called a *ture,* went to work in the fields each day. When they arrived they put down their instruments and stuck the pole in the ground before starting work. At the end of day, the pole would be raised again and accompanied back to the village by music. It was very important that the flag should never touch the ground and that any movement of the pole was accompanied by music.

In the evenings the village would often hold a contest, called a *pankut,* at which the musicians would accompany dancing, or just play more complicated music for their audience. The instruments which were always used consisted of two gongs (a little, very loud one called a *kwaenggwari,* which is struck with a wooden mallet and is the leader's instrument, and a larger one called a *ching,* which is struck with a soft-headed stick) and two drums (the *puk,* a double-headed barrel drum, and the *changgo,* which is an hourglass drum with a thicker skin on one side than the other, the thinner one being struck with a bamboo stick and the thicker one with either the hand or a mallet).

Unfortunately, rapid economic growth and mechanization since about 1970 have caused the traditional *ture* to die out, and the farmers' music in its original form has gone with it. But Kim Duk Soo has studied all the rhythms from different regions and different generations and uses them in the performances given by Samul Nori. Strictly speaking it is chamber music rather than farmers' music, although the group don't actually create pieces but put the original rhythms into a new and exciting order.

Kim Duk Soo and Suzanna went on to explain that folk music in Korea is divided into three forms. The first, *nongak,* encompasses tilling and planting songs for men, with the band accompanying them, spinning songs for women, which are unaccompanied, and weeding songs for boys and youths, which are also unaccompanied. It also includes workers' songs and fishermen's songs. It is *nongak* on which Samul Nori's music is based. The other two forms are folk songs and shamanist music, of which I was to discover more later.

I was lucky to arrive just as the group were beginning their daily routine and watched them do stretching exercises, then spiritual preparation based on the rhythm of breathing, which seems to be more important in Korean music than pulse, upon which Western music is based. The group then stood up and started a dance exercise, with Kim Duk Soo playing the *kwaenggwari* and another man playing a *changgo.* They all put on hats with ribbons on long wire, which I discovered are called *sangmo,* and then, holding small tabors called *sogos,* they cartwheeled and danced around the room, sending their ribbons spinning in circles. Then everyone picked up a *changgo* and sat on the floor. Suzanna gave me a *changgo* too and invited me to join in as they started to work on different rhythms. At first it was easy as the rhythms were fairly simple, but as it got faster and the rhythms became extremely complex I couldn't follow them any more and sat back to watch. It was extraordinarily exciting to feel the vibration from eighteen or so *changgos* being hit as hard as possible on a wooden floor, and my fellow visitors were complaining about their ears distorting because it was so loud. As the drumming got faster and more energetic the musicians moved with the rhythm, and I realized that the use of the body is very important in this style of music.

I decided that I really wanted to learn to play the *changgo* properly, so Kim Duk Soo kindly spent some time teaching me. The most difficult thing was holding the drum, as I had to sit cross-legged on the floor and grip it with my feet. I found this very uncomfortable, especially as I was wearing tight jeans!

When I left Samul Nori, I knew I had to buy a *changgo*. This was easier said than done, however, as the instrument shop I was told to go to was situated somewhere in a network of back streets and the lack of street names meant that the poor taxi driver had only a vague idea of the area. So I had to jump out and search for the shop on foot. Having failed to find it, I asked a passing citizen if he knew of any good percussion shops, and fortunately he directed me to the one I was looking for!

I was amazed to find myself in a tiny room absolutely crammed with percussion instruments and paraphernalia. Different types of stick and mallet were jammed into pots and brightly coloured tassels waited to be hung on various instruments. Stacked up in the corner were several *changgos,* and I spent some time discussing the merits of the various instruments before picking one that looked strong and well-made. I asked the shopkeeper to replace the cowhide skins with better-quality goatskin, and it was very interesting to watch how he threaded the rope from skin to skin to pull them tight. He also slipped little leather pieces on to the ropes so that the tension could be increased and decreased. He gave me a case in which to put my *changgo,* and a collection of bamboo sticks; after rummaging around to find the right amount of cash (no credit cards here!) I went out into the evening clutching my new acquisition.

Have *changgo*, will travel – but where? South-east to a little village called Hahoe (pronounced Hahway), which my book assured me was famous for its masked dance, known as *Byulshin kut.* It is also renowned as being a remote village united in its Confucian beliefs, emphasizing devotion to peace, justice and the family. So the next morning I set off back to Kimpo Airport and the Domestic Terminal to catch the flight to a place called Yechon. I had some difficulty finding this on my map, as it is not a large town and I couldn't imagine why it had an airport.

Just over half an hour after take-off we were descending into what looked like a solid range of mountains where I didn't see how we could possibly land. Then suddenly I saw a huge landing strip on the only flat stretch of earth for miles around. All was revealed as we taxied past a collection of sleek, lowering military aircraft, some of which took off terrifyingly over our heads as we walked off the plane. The terminal is tiny, and civilian aircraft are probably only there on sufferance.

Our taxi driver missed the turning and we had to retrace our steps, until finally we drove along a dirt road beside a beautiful stretch of river and arrived at Hahoe. This was a shock. As I turned from contemplating the magnificent cliffs on the other side of the river and the elegant curve of water that almost encloses the village, I found myself looking at a tacky hut with rickety tables and benches in front of it and a banner proclaiming the wonders of Coke. Was this really the well-preserved Confucian village? Venturing further, I was met by a charming man who turned out to be Kim Dong Pyo, the resident mask-maker. He kindly invited me to his house and we entered a traditional cottage, removing our shoes at the door as is the custom in Korea. I found myself in a small room with linoleum on the floor and a child sitting on a bench at the table watching television. Mrs Kim put the kettle on the electric stove and made us a cup of instant coffee while Mr Kim invited me to sit on the sofa as he explained the story of the masked dance.

The legend is that seven hundred years ago many disasters struck the village. A young man named Huh, a noble's son, had a dream in which God appeared and promised him that, if he made twelve masks which were worn at a *kut* (a religious ceremony), the disasters would disappear. However, God cautioned Huh that he must not let anyone see the masks until they were finished. The young man locked himself into a room and got on with the job. It took a long time. He had finished eleven masks and had embarked upon the twelfth when a girl who was in love with him decided that she had to know what he was doing. So she made a hole in the paper which formed the window, and looked in. God was predictably angry, and Huh died by vomiting blood. The twelfth mask was complete except for its jaw; it is called *Imae tal,* which means 'foolish man mask'.

The Hahoe *Byulshin kut* was enacted with Huh's masks after his death and has been performed ever since, not annually, but usually every three to five years or even ten years — in fact when some kind of disaster occurs. The villagers say that the success of the *kut* is proved by the fact that the village is now seven hundred years old — so it must work!

Koreans used to believe that there were gods for everything — a kitchen god, a bedroom god, a living room god and so on — but most important was the village god, to whom each village builds a shrine. Some people say that the *Byulshin kut* was intended to appease the village god, and the ceremony was also performed if someone received a revelation from this god (usually the high priest of the shrine, who, as soon as he received the revelation, would visit the shrine and find that, however hard it rained, his fire would not be extinguished as it was protected).

In 1928, however, the occupying Japanese stopped this tradition in their quest to extinguish Korean culture. There were no more *Byulshin kuts* until a group of young people tried to stage one about thirty years ago. They found that they couldn't do it all — only the play with the masks. Although outsiders call it a masked dance, it used to be a religious ceremony and therefore a *kut;* but now it is only the play element which is performed, and so its character has changed. It is now merely a way of preserving Korean culture — the masked dance was designated a National Treasure in 1965.

The centuries-old village of Hahoe was founded on Confucian beliefs that stress the values of justice, peace and family relationships. Nowadays it is a tourist honeypot.

Overleaf: The masked dance or Byulshin kut is an ancient religious ceremony in honour of the local village god. The wonderfully carved masks, copies of the twelve, according to legend, made by the young nobleman Huh, reflect expressions typical of different social levels in Yi Dynasty society.

The masks are wonderfully carved: each one reflects a Korean expression typical of a particular social level in Yi Dynasty society; this dynasty lasted from 1392 to 1910 and was heavily influenced by Confucian thought introduced from China. Originally the masks were considered holy, and sacrifices had to be made to them before and after they were worn. One of the reasons for the superstition surrounding them was that they appeared to reflect the wearer's emotion – if he laughed, so did his mask. This is because of the clever way the jaws are attached: if the wearer lowers his head, for instance, the mask frowns, and if he raises his head the mask laughs. It was believed that if a mask was touched arbitrarily a disaster would happen – *tal nanda* is a Korean expression reflecting this. Nine of the original masks are preserved in the Seoul National Museum; and although three are lost, two of another kind are also exhibited there. The masks continue to be carved exactly like the originals, but only those are considered sacred now. When I asked how often the masks have to be replaced, Mr Kim told me that they last a long time and are only replaced when it is considered that the expression has faded and no longer looks like the original.

I was taken through the village to a nobleman's house belonging to the family of a famous President, Yu: the large houses with tiled roofs, it was explained to me, belonged to nobles, while the smaller houses with thatched roofs belonged to their servants. The masked dance was performed in front of the President's house to the accompaniment of the four-piece farmers' band which I had found out about earlier. The dance was very colourful and consisted of several different scenes, mostly mocking the ruling classes. The *Yangban* (nobles) must have been extremely tolerant – they paid for the villagers to enjoy this dance, although they never attended themselves. They must have been aware, however, that the dances were directed against them.

I wish I could say I enjoyed my trip to Hahoe, but to be honest the tackiness depressed me. Everywhere I turned there was either a café or a souvenir shop, and the signs of modern life, from electricity to mobile phones, detracted from the authenticity I was expecting. Although the dance was interesting, it was clearly a reconstruction rather than a living thing in its own right.

I left the village to travel through spectacular mountains and lake scenery to Kyongju, near the south-east coast. This was the site of the capital of the ancient Silla Dynasty, which grew to rule the whole of modern Korea during the Unified Silla period between 668 and 935. During its golden age it was an extremely sophisticated culture, attracting artists, musicians and writers. As a result it was declared one of the ten major ancient history sites in the world by the UNESCO conference in Thailand in 1979.

On arriving at Kyongju I was driven to yet another large, impersonal hotel, but this time facing a huge and beautiful lake. My balcony was covered by a fly screen – which was just as well, because the midges would have had a fine time otherwise – but the view of the setting sun was spectacular. The next morning I met Professor Hwang Byung-kee, one of Korea's most eminent musicians. Professor Hwang graduated from Seoul National

An inquisitive fellow traveller.

Overleaf: Professor Hwang Byung-kee on kayagum
and Evelyn on changgo, *by the shore of the beautiful
Anapchi Lake at Kyongju.*

University as a lawyer before turning to music, and he is now a composer and eminent *kayagum* player and teacher. The *kayagum* is a twelve-stringed, zither-like instrument with a beautiful, soft, sweet tone, and he told me that there are pictures of it dating back to the Silla period. Indeed, the name probably comes from a place called Kaya, which was eventually absorbed into the region ruled by the Unified Silla Dynasty.

Professor Hwang took me to see the extraordinary tombs of the Silla kings, in an area known as Tumulus Park. There are more than twenty large and small tombs all buried under varying-sized mounds, the largest being 75 feet (23 metres) tall. While we walked around the park, the professor told me how Silla culture had differed from that of the Yi Dynasty. The Confucian influence in the Yi Dynasty had demanded that women should be veiled and never show their bodies. Women really had no place in the Confucian order except as a biological necessity and as servants – with the exception of the notorious *kisaeng*, who were well-educated prostitutes similar to Japanese geisha girls. The Sillas, by contrast, had an open society. Women wore flimsy clothes through which one could see their breasts, sex was free and easy, and the ornaments were very elaborate. The people combined their indigenous art with foreign influences to create something from which, even in still pictures and architecture, we can extrapolate movement.

Interestingly, these liberal attitudes were probably as closely associated with Silla religious views as the Yi restrictions were with Confucianism. The Sillas had a strong shamanist tradition, and the elaborate and intricately made royal crowns which I saw later in the Kyongju National Museum bear a remarkable similarity to Siberian shaman head-dresses (the priestly cult of shamanism, about which I was soon to discover more, originally spread to Korea from Siberia). The Sillas embraced Buddhism as well, which is a free-thinking religion; I was interested to see that much of Silla art has an Indian feel, and of course Buddhism originated in that country.

Professor Hwang explained that his country has absorbed and blended a number of religious traditions. They stretch from shamanism, which has been in Korea for at least five thousand years, through Buddhism and Confucianism to Christianity, with overtones of Islam and other lesser-known religions. Religious freedom is now enshrined in the law, and various religious practices which had been banned from time to time during history have all been reinstated.

The various faiths have played an important part in the development of Korea's culture, and the people's continual search for harmony, both in their own lives and in the world which they inhabit, has encouraged a unique fusion between religions. Thus elements of shamanist art may be seen in Buddhist temples blending with hints of Confucianism and Taoism. The mysticism of shamanism sits comfortably beside the gentle liberalism and great art of Buddhism, while the Confucian moral code is ingrained in the modern Korean even though the old order was demolished over seventy years ago.

Shamanism encompasses the worship of thousands of spirits, many of them ill disposed towards those still living. Objects of worship include not only celestial bodies but rocks, trees and mountains as well. The religion's priests, or shamans, are of two types in Korea: the Saesumodang and the Kungshimo. The former, who are found throughout southern Korea, inherit through the male line. They can only marry into another shamanic family, so all the girls in such a family study dances and music with their mothers from a very young age. Once they are married, they continue their studies with their mothers-in-law until they are ready to assist in progressively difficult ceremonies. Meanwhile their husbands will be playing traditional instruments during ceremonies *(kut).* The whole family or village will ask the *mudang,* as the Saesumodang girl becomes through marriage, for whatever they want. She is considered to be a god already, through inheritance, and there is therefore no need for her to enter a trance as the Kungshimo *mudang* must.

The future Kungshimo shaman, found mostly in the north, receives the holy spirit suddenly, usually following sickness. She (it is usually a female) goes to another shaman and enters a teacher/disciple relationship similar to a courtesy mother/daughter relationship. The future shaman usually has some presentiment or omen that she will receive the spirit – her sickness can't be cured by medicine, so she goes to the fortune-teller/shaman who drives out the ill spirit. Then she in turn becomes a shaman. After she has been through a private ceremony, a *nerimkut,* she can explain to the people what sort of holy spirit she has received.

In both forms of shamanism the content of the ceremonies is essentially the same, but the style of dancing, singing and performing is different. Both begin the ritual with songs invoking the spirits, and then dance a welcome to the holy spirit. In Saesumodang the holy spirit sits on the altar, but in Kungshimo the *mudang* gains supernatural powers once she becomes possessed by a spirit in the course of the *kut.* These powers are demonstrated by feats such as dancing barefoot on a pair of knife blades without shedding blood. In both ceremonies a long piece of cloth is knotted to represent the spirit's psychological wounds, which the unknotting of the cloth will heal. A shamanist *kut* can last for hours, if not days, and is still attended in times of trouble by many people who profess not to be believers when life is flowing smoothly!

Buddhism arrived in Korea in AD 372 in the Koguryo Kingdom (the source of the name 'Korea'). It spread like wildfire except in the Silla Kingdom, which did not accept it until 527. The country follows the Mahayana (meaning 'greater vehicle') branch of the religion, which allows many bodhisattvas to accompany the Buddha in the thousands of temples throughout the land. Bodhisattvas are deities who have decided to defer their entrance to Nirvana – a kind of Buddhist heaven – in the interests of assisting those still living to strive for personal salvation. This is achieved through acceptance of the Four Noble Truths of Buddha's enlightenment and following the Noble Eightfold Path, which forms three categories of morality, wisdom and concentration.

Buddhism suffered a sharp decline in 1392 when Confucianism was declared the state religion. Confucianism had arrived in Korea at about the same time as Buddhism, along with other Chinese beliefs such as Taoism. It is not strictly a religion, more a code of ethics, as there is no divine power to worship. Despite this, it became the overwhelming discipline until the end of the Yi Dynasty in 1910.

Confucius taught that society should value five relationships – ruler/subjects, husband/wife, father/son, elder/younger brothers, and friendship. The social order was paramount, with the aristocracy striving to reach the highest ranks of officialdom through intense study of the Confucian texts and the creation of outstanding poems and exquisite calligraphy.

Since the upheaval of the Japanese invasion of the country in 1910 Confucian concepts have become less influential, a process accelerated by the fragmentation of the close-knit family system. But the customs, thought patterns and habits have not really disappeared. Buddhism and shamanism, on the other hand, have enjoyed a tremendous revival since the end of the Korean War, and Christianity (which first entered the country, tentatively, in 1592 but didn't take off until the middle of the nineteenth century) had become increasingly popular.

As with all Korean culture, the country's music, too, is imbued with a strong religious element. Professor Hwang told me that his own compositions are frequently based on the spirit of the Silla era, the remains of which surrounded us, and he suggested that we should visit Anapchi Lake, which had been built in 674 during the reign of King Munmu-wang after the unification of the Korean peninsula. Here a number of pavilions, including the large Imhaejon, had been built around a lake which contained three central islands, while to the north and east are twelve hills; Professor Hwang explained that this composition reflects the Shinson (Taoist) philosophy. We took our instruments with us and the professor taught me to play the *changgo* part of his duet for *kayagum* and *changgo* called 'Chimhyang-moo'. This translates as 'Silent Fragrance Dance', and was inspired by the figure of Buddha in a temple as well as the spirit of Silla art.

I relished the challenge of getting to grips with an entirely new musical form – the use of the *changgo* here was entirely different from that in the farmers' music. It was fascinating to see what Professor Hwang could do with the *kayagum* as well – by changing the pressure on the strings, which are made of wound silk, he could vary the pitch of the notes in an unusual way. I discovered that variable pitch is an important feature of Korean music, and it was later suggested to me that this was part of the Oriental preference for things to be obscured rather than clear and open as we Westerners prefer. White space is important to them as well – both in art and as pauses in music.

Afterwards we went to look at Silla antiques in the Kyongju National Museum, in particular the sacred bell of King Songdok-wang, which hangs outside. At about 12.3 feet (3.75 metres) high it is the largest of its kind in the Orient, and was cast in 771. The story goes that when it was first cast it would not ring, so it was melted down again. The chief priest of the temple where the bell was being cast had a vision in which he was told to throw a little child into the molten metal to make it ring properly. This they did, would you believe, and when the bell was finally rung it produced a sound like the Korean word for

'Mummy' – *Emille* – reflecting the child's cries when it was sacrificed. To this day the bell is popularly known as the Emille Bell. It used to be struck thirty-three times every New Year's Eve, but it is now considered too delicate to be played; I was, however, given a recording of it. Professor Hwang told me that he had actually struck the bell once, and the sound it made was truly exquisite.

Inside the museum we saw an ancient clay pot which was probably used by farmers to store seed, as it was obviously a fertility symbol of some kind. The collection of figures surrounding it includes some having sex and one naked pregnant woman playing a *kayagum*!

Before he left, Professor Hwang told me that I must be sure to see Pulguksa Temple and the Sokkulam Buddha while I was in Kyongju. So I went up to the temple and was kindly offered a bed for the night, an opportunity which I felt I could not miss.

I was allocated a small bare room with a roll of bedding which I could lay out when I went to sleep. First I went to look around the temple, and was overcome with its beauty and serenity. Unfortunately I had missed the main evening ceremony at 6.30 and had only a short time left before the monks retired for the night at nine o'clock, but I spent the remaining time admiring the way in which the construction of the buildings harmonized with the mountains and trees behind. The temple has stood at the foot of Tohamsan mountain since 751. At that time it was one of the largest Buddhist temples, with more than eighty buildings, and was the centre of Silla Buddhism. The Japanese reduced it to ashes in 1593, but the principal buildings were reconstructed and it was completely restored between 1969 and 1973. The site contains two very important stone pagodas and various other relics, but what impressed me the most was the peace and timelessness of it all. I felt I could stay there for ever.

Life is not like that, however, and I found sleeping on the floor with a thin mattress and hard pillow was not the most restful experience! I was quite pleased to get up at 4 a.m. to climb the mountain and watch the spectacular sunrise, with the mist slowly thinning as the sky reddened and glowed across the mountain ranges and beyond them the sea. Once it was completely light, I walked on up the mountain to the Sokkulam Grotto, which is a cave temple contemporary with the main temple. I had been told that the stone figures in the grotto represent the best sculpture of the Unified Silla Dynasty and indeed of all Korea, so I entered the little pavilion which fronts the cave with great anticipation. Beyond the small antechamber I came to the main hall, where my eyes were drawn immediately to the Buddha which dominates the rotunda. He is 11.4 feet (3.48 metres) high and sits facing east with the most serene and benevolent smile on his face that I think I have ever seen. The stone seems curiously alive and his draped garments flow around him. I found it hard to drag my eyes away from him to look at the many other figures, all beautifully carved – the Buddha dominates and draws one back to him again and again.

As I walked back down the mountain again I noticed something I had missed on the way up – a full-sized replica of the Emille Bell, cast in 1991! I asked if I could hit it. Every-

Pages 136-8: Pulguksa Temple, Kyongju.
Built in AD 531 and extended in 751, the temple was destroyed
by the Japanese in the late sixteenth century but has been
completely restored in the last few decades.

Decorative detail on the Pulguksa Temple.

one laughed and said I could if I must, so I did. I understood their laughter then – it has the most dreadful sound, not at all like its illustrious original. Still, I can't help being pleased – at least we know they didn't sacrifice another poor little child!

Now that I had heard so much about it I wanted to explore Buddhism further. The most precious Buddhist possessions, I was told, were at the temple of Haeinsa, about two hours' drive from Kyongju, so I bade a reluctant farewell to Pulguska and Sokkulam and set off again, with my driver.

The huge expressway took me through a heavily industrialized area, and as we passed the large city of Taegu I couldn't help noticing the huddles of shacks where the very poor were living close to the road. It was a sad sight, repeated all over the world – even, these days, in London. We swept on, halting only briefly at the toll gate, until we came to the turn-off to Haeinsa.

From here we started to climb until we entered Kayasan National Park, where the narrow road twisted and turned beside a stream with mountains towering on both sides. Eventually we stopped beside a building which contained shops and a restaurant, and then I joined the throng toiling up the steep path towards the temple. Haeinsa is famous principally because it contains the Tripitaka Koreana. The Tripitaka (or three baskets) is the Buddhist canon containing three important collections of writings: the Sutra Pitaka, a collection of discourses primarily between Buddha and other people; the Vinaya Pitaka, a code of more than 225 rules of monastic discipline; and the Abhidharma Pitaka, which contains philosophical, psychological and doctrinal discussions and classifications. The Tripitaka Koreana consists of 81 258 wood blocks, dating from the thirteenth century, which are the most complete Buddhist scriptures in the world.

By the time I had been walking uphill for twenty minutes, however, I wondered whether I really wanted to see this treasure and I understood why there were so many way-side stalls offering refreshment. But eventually I arrived at a shrine with a flight of steps leading off to the right which looked hopeful. The steps turned out to be the final killer – if the path was steep, the steps were steeper, and I wondered how on earth the monks could climb them in their long robes. At last, much out of breath, I emerged into a huge court-yard where my eye was drawn to a large open pavilion with lots of instruments inside – and several cars in front! Apparently there was a road after all for those who had permission to use it, but we poor pilgrims had to walk! I decided I would investigate the instrument house on the way back, and crossed an inner courtyard surrounded by a number of new buildings in my search for the famous wood blocks. I was fascinated to see the construction of the long building which houses them. It has no windows – only two layers of slatted open frames along both sides of the wood and lath structure. The purpose is clearly to let the fresh mountain air circulate freely inside the building, which keeps the printing blocks at an even temperature. The building is quite dark inside, so that the wood will not be damaged by sunlight, and the blocks themselves are kept on strong shelves, well off the ground, just like in any other library. I was able to see some blocks close up, which was fascinating. Each one

has twenty-three fourteen-letter lines on each side, and there are apparently 6708 volumes in 1501 categories.

I discovered that there are two other buildings in the same style but smaller, containing 2835 more printing blocks which were carved between 1098 and 1349 during the Koryo period. They include the works of several famous monks. Examples of some of the prints were on display and I could not resist buying a couple which had beautiful drawings on them, as well as the artistic calligraphy which is considered very important.

Haeinsa seemed much bigger than Pulguksa – the main shrine is enormous, and although it too is in harmony with its spectacular surroundings I did not find it had the same atmosphere. I felt no great desire to linger there and instead made my way back to the large instrument house. In contrast to the little one at Pulguksa which held only a beautifully decorated drum, I found that this one contained a huge bell, similar to the Emille Bell but not on quite the same scale; a large drum (not decorated at all) seated on a wooden frame; a hanging fish; and a curly sheet of metal with pretty ornamentation on it, which is called a cloud plate.

I had still not managed to witness a full Buddhist ceremony, which only occurs twice a day, at 4 a.m. and 6.30 p.m. I could have stayed for the morning one at Pulguksa, but if I had done so I would have missed the sunrise on the mountain. Since, however, I was still interested in seeing the instruments in use I was advised that my best bet would be to go to Songgwangsa Temple. This is the only temple in Korea where foreign monks are allowed to live, so my chances of finding an English-speaker to explain the ceremony were high.

I walked down the mountain again to find my driver, and as I did so I wondered whether to try one of the snacks on offer at the stalls. On my journey so far I had found that I really missed the sandwich culture in which we Westerners live. Quick lunches do not appear to be generally available in Korea, where one sits down to a meal of several different dishes eaten with metal chopsticks. One of the side dishes is always the national dish, *kimchi.* This is Chinese leaf which has been pickled in strong spices, including chilli, and can be stored for months. It is served cold and usually lifts the roof off your mouth, so the plain boiled sticky rice which is also served at every meal has a dual purpose: it takes the heat out of the spicy food as well as filling you up!

It was a long way from Haeinsa to Songgwangsa, so I stayed overnight in a town called Namwon. One of my fellow guests at the hotel was Yu Young-dae, a professor of Korean literature at Chonju University. From him I discovered that Namwon is the centre of another form of Korean music, called *pansori,* which is a sort of one-man opera. I knew that I should have to return here to explore further after my trip to Songgwangsa. Professor Yu,

Opposite: The Sukkolam Buddha at Pulguksa and its companion figures represent the finest stone sculpture of the Unified Silla Dynasty.

Overleaf: As in most Far Eastern countries, rice, grown in flooded paddy fields, is the staple which is served at every meal.

a *pansori* specialist, promised that he would arrange for me to meet people who would show me the living music I was after.

As I travelled on to Songgwangsa, at one stage we were driving on a road that crossed and recrossed a huge lake called Sungjuho. The sun was shining and the reflection of the mountains in the still water made me think of Switzerland. I had not realized before I came that Korea would be so mountainous. I knew that there was a long spine of mountainous country running down the eastern side of the peninsula, but I had found that even areas that my map indicated as flat contained interesting scenery with plenty of hills.

Once again, I discovered that the temple I was visiting was situated up a mountain in a National Park with the car park some way further down. I understood by this time that mountains are extremely important in the philosophy of the Korean people, which is why all the temples are on mountains and the hillsides are dotted with grave mounds. This time I spotted the road, which went up through a wood yard, but I walked just the same – fortunately it wasn't quite as steep as the path to Haeinsa! Songgwangsa actually had a café right by the entrance to the temple; but I resolutely passed it by, and entered the large gate to see the splendidly painted four heavenly kings who guard the four cardinal directions of the universe, one of whom always holds a lute-like instrument. Inside the 'Extensive Pines Temples', as Songgwangsa means, there was a large instrument house like the one at Haeinsa; but the drum here was suspended and also magnificently painted like that at Pulguksa.

I was met by Chi-su, a monk who had lived in England for a time and who gave me a conducted tour in English. I had been rather surprised by the lack of English-speakers in Korea in view of the American influence on the country since the Korean War, and it was a relief to be able to communicate directly instead of through an interpreter. I was particularly interested in one building which had a frieze of the Buddhist story known as 'Catch Bull at Four' painted on the outside. The first five frames of the story were at the front of the building, with a boat-like wooden object underneath. Chi-su explained that the 'boat' was a hollowed out tree trunk containing rice for visitors. We then walked round to the back of the building to find the last five frames of the story. I was rather confused because the pictures along the side were from a different story altogether!

When I looked inside the main shrine I was fascinated to see that the central seated Buddha, a large gilt figure, was flanked by two standing and several seated bodhisattvas with hundreds of small gilt figures carved in rows behind. In front of the altar was a little table with a silver handbell and the wooden *moktak* which I had discovered all the monks strike during prayers. These small instruments have a handle and then an acorn-shaped, hollow body, the bottom end of which is split up to the middle, where there is a hole on each side. The monks strike the *moktak* with a wooden stick which looks rather like a thin, elongated skittle.

Chi-su explained that Songgwangsa is the centre for the Korean version of Zen Buddhism, Chogye Son, and since 1969 it has been designated a complete training centre.

This is why foreigners are allowed to live here. The Son monks spend three months in retreat, meditating, and then for the next three months remain in the temple but are given a little more freedom. I asked whether all the monks would be in one shrine for the evening ceremony. Chi-su explained that according to the rules there must be at least one monk at every shrine (of which there are several) during prayers, and that the temple contained managing monks and students as well as the Son monks, who would not be at prayers; but there would be at least forty monks at the main shrine. I also asked about the instruments used in the ceremony and was told that some would be in the instrument house and others in the main shrine. I wondered whether I could play any of them, but their religious significance means that they are only allowed to be touched by monks and during ceremonies – except for the *moktak,* which Chi-su showed me how to use.

The ceremony started with the huge bell being hit thirty-three times with a log swinging on chains. After this the beautifully painted drum was beaten for between five and ten minutes, and then it was the turn of the fish. I was told that the fish must be struck 108 times (33 and 108 are significant figures in Buddhism), but as it is very difficult to keep track when counting to such a high number, the fish is struck in three different rhythmic sequences which total 108. After the fish, the cloud plate was beaten, also in three rhythmic sequences, and then the rest of the ceremony was performed inside the shrine. It was very moving, even though I could not understand the words. The chanting of the monks accompanied by the *moktaks,* the little silver bell and a large gong, beside which there was a huge *moktak,* created a devotional atmosphere which transcended individual religious beliefs.

Back in Namwon, Professor Yu had been very busy. He had organized a meeting for me with one of the city's most famous daughters, Ahn Suk-Son. Now in her mid-forties, Mrs Ahn is acclaimed as probably the best *pansori* singer in the country. She is an attractive, charismatic lady with tremendous personality, and although she now lives in Seoul she had come back to Namwon at Professor Yu's request. It transpired that he too had been born in Namwon, and obviously had excellent contacts with his fellow citizens.

Professor Yu and Mrs Ahn explained that *pansori* originated from the *Ssikkimkut,* a shaman ceremony for sending the spirit to a better place. There are two aspects to this ceremony, religious and artistic. *Pansori* removed the religious aspect and reinforced the artistic side. The original repertoire was based on twelve stories, although only five of these are still used. Others have been introduced, some with a political focus, others with social, romantic or pornographic themes. The singer, who can be either male or female, sings, narrates and dances the story alone except for a single accompanist, who plays the *puk* drum. The performance can last for many hours, and it is the drummer's job to stimulate the singer with vocal remarks as well as beating his instrument – not only the skin but on the wood as well. This art form started off as entertainment for the lower classes, but about a hundred years ago the Yi Dynasty nobility decided to patronize performers, and *pansori* thus became more refined and beautiful.

At the Songgwangsa or 'Extensive Pines' temple, the main centre for the Korean form of Zen Buddhism.

Son monks at Songgwangsa beat the great suspended drum
at the end of the day.

One reason that Namwon is the centre of the *pansori* world is that the most popular story is set here. Namwon's geographical location, including the pen shape of one of the local mountains, has long been considered auspicious for the raising of literary people, so it is no surprise that this is based upon the town.

The story concerns a young girl called Choonhyang – 'Fragrance of Spring' – who was the daughter of a *kisaeng*. This meant that she could follow her mother by becoming a courtesan to the upper classes or *Yangban,* but not that she could marry one of them. Briefly, Mong Yong, the young son of the most important local official, saw Choonhyang in the park of Kwanghalloo and fell deeply in love with her. They got married, but he didn't dare tell his father. So when he was sent off to Seoul to complete his studies for his examinations to become a government official (the Confucian *Yangban* ideal), he left his wife behind in Namwon, promising to return one day. A new official who subsequently replaced Mong Yong's father wanted Choonhyang to become his mistress, and when the girl refused he had her thrown in prison. Here she languished for a long time, getting weaker and weaker but refusing to compromise her position as a faithful wife, while the new official caused great unhappiness all round. Meanwhile, Mong Yong had won first prize in the literary contest before the king and been created an Ussa, the king's personal inspector who roamed the country checking that lower officials were doing their job fairly. When the young Ussa returned to Namwon he discovered this sorry state of affairs and ordered his underlings to meet him in Kwanghan Pavilion in Kwanghalloo Park. From here they stormed the official's residence and imprisoned him. Choonhyang was released and reunited with her husband, who was now in a position to acknowledge her publicly as his wife. We presume they lived happily ever after.

Professor Yu and Mrs Ahn took me to see Kwanghalloo Park, which is one of only two Yi Dynasty classical gardens left and contains the supposed birthplace and shrine to Choonhyang. It is a very pretty place with the classic Taoist three islands on a lake (representing three mountains inhabited by Taoist immortal men), with three bowers on each, and a graceful bridge called Ozakyo, supposed to be formed by crows and magpies, where legend has it that two people living in heaven can meet once a year. There are also hundreds of holy fish – Koi carp – in the lake. Inside the shrine there is a fascinating portrait of Choonhyang in which her hair is not visible. I was told that this is so we cannot tell whether at this time Choonhyang was a young girl, with her hair plaited down her back, or a married woman with her hair dressed up on her head. Either way she is clearly revered, both as the model of a faithful wife and as a girl who managed to rise above her station, and has been for at least sixty years. In her honour an annual nationwide *pansori* competition is held here, which Ahn Suk-Son won in 1988.

Mrs Ahn told me of the belief that a *pansori* singer has to practise for at least fourteen years in a forest or under a waterfall to perfect the voice and art before performing. The

Ahn Suk-Son, regarded as the best pansori *singer in Korea.*

theory is that when the voice can penetrate the waterfall, it is perfect. She used to practise for at least six hours a day until she was in her late thirties, but now she feels she needs to devote less time to it. The technique is clearly different from Western opera singing, and *pansori* singers feel that constant practice strengthens their vocal chords. I was interested to test the waterfall theory and she laughingly agreed to take me to a waterfall where she had practised, and to look at Choonhyang's burial mound at the same time.

So we drove into the huge Chirisan National Park and penetrated deep into the mountain. Here we found Choonhyang's grave; at its base is a famous *pansori* waterfall which has a natural flat rock on either side of the river. Many performances are given here, with the singer on the far side of the river and the audience on the near side. Mrs Ahn wanted to show me another waterfall, however, so we drove on. Eventually we stopped and scrambled along a rocky path until we came to a splendid high waterfall with a flat rock in front. Mrs Ahn walked cautiously over to the rock and demonstrated a section of the Choonhyang story for me. It was terrific and her voice penetrated the noise of the water quite easily! I was amazed at the way she uses her voice and the complex ornaments required. I understood now why it takes so long to learn the music, particularly as it is all passed on orally from master to pupil, and not written down.

That evening a banquet had been arranged, which I was invited to attend. When I arrived I found a table just a few inches above the floor, on which we all had to sit cross-legged. The table was absolutely groaning with food, and I counted at least twenty side dishes on each section. An area at the top of the room had been cleared and I noticed that some of my fellow guests were wearing traditional costume. Professor Yu explained to me that they were all professors of music and were going to play for us during the meal. We were very honoured, because Korean music is not supposed to be ruined by people eating through it, but the Director of the National Folk Music Institute in Namwon had given us special dispensation.

We ate our way through the amazing quantity of food before us, although I'm afraid I passed when it came to the raw fish and I wasn't so keen on the spicy pickled vegetables either. Sitting cross-legged was beginning to become extremely uncomfortable for me by the time the musicians rose and went to perform. Fortunately we had to sit back against the wall so that everybody could see, so I had a chance to stretch my legs! We enjoyed a performance by a *taegum* (a kind of flute) player with a *changgo,* followed by a delightful performance on the *ajaeng* – a smaller, seven-stringed version of Professor Hwang's *kayagum,* – also with *changgo* accompaniment. The drummer then swopped to a *puk* and a lady got up to sing us some *pansori*. I was enchanted by the audience's reaction. Here indeed was living

The Ssikkimkut *was originally a religious ceremony which lasted many hours and centred on washing rituals. It has now been revived in a shortened version which can be performed on the stage. Here, in a ceremony on Chindo, a musician plays a gong.*

music. The classical story notwithstanding, the singer and her audience interacted strongly with each other, and not just the drummer but everyone else egged her on, commented and exclaimed. Here was an art form obviously deeply loved by everybody present and the performer gave so much in response. I was really thrilled to have experienced this. We all applauded enthusiastically when she finished and then I found all eyes were on me! Would I go and play the *puk* with the drummer on the *changgo?* What could I say? Of course! Someone held the *puk* up for me and the drummer offered a rhythm – and off we went, improvising like mad. Once again I could feel the audience's enthusiasm and it was enormous fun. We went through several different rhythmic patterns and, as always, the language of music overcame all barriers.

Eventually we both returned to our seats and I thought this would be the end of the evening, but no. There was another course! I couldn't believe my eyes as yet more food was put in front of us – no one had warned me that the banquet we had gorged ourselves on earlier was only a starter. It finished eventually, however, so I warmly thanked my host for a wonderful evening and returned to my hotel. The night was young, however, in the eyes of the music community. I received an invitation to go to Professor Yu's room, where I found eighteen people settling down with two large carrier bags full of beer. After all the rice wine that had been swilling around at the banquet, the men at least were getting fairly merry by now – women are exempt from the traditional hospitable habit of passing empty drinking bowls and filling them until everyone is under the table. We had a ball. Everyone was encouraged to play everyone else's instruments, all the guests were dancing and singing *pansori* (some of it they refused to translate, but I could sense it was very rude!) and the party went on for hours. If I was looking for living music, then I need look no further. This was their traditional music and they really loved it.

All my travelling around had worn me out and eventually I excused myself, but I was told the next morning that they had gone on well into the night. After one look at the hungover faces at breakfast I believed them. How could they stomach their traditional breakfast, which consists of the same spicy food as lunch and dinner, I couldn't imagine. Even smelling it put me off my fried egg and toast.

Although I felt very close to what I had come for, I realized that all the links led back to one thing which I had not yet found: shamanism. Farmers' music, upon which Samul Nori's performances are based, followed the shaman spirit pole. The Hahoe masked dance was originally the *Byulshin kut,* a shaman ceremony to ward off disaster. Silla art was based on shaman art as well as Buddhist art. *Pansori* came from a shaman ceremony called *Ssikkimkut.* Professor Yu told me to go to the south-western island of Chindo to find the *Ssikkimkut,* so I said farewell to my new friends and set off on my travels again.

A woman holds a pole swathed in a white cloth during
the final part of the Ssikkimkut *ceremony held on the beach*
on Chindo.

I travelled by train to the port of Mokpo and then hired a taxi to Chindo. We wended our way around the coast until eventually a signpost told us that Chindo lay ahead. I wanted to cross to the island by boat. This puzzled my driver, who pointed out that the residents of Chindo were rightly very proud of their new bridge; but being a mad foreigner I insisted on doing it the traditional way!

Safely reunited on the island, we drove past hamlets of traditional houses nestling at the base of hills with rice paddies stretched out before them, and on to the unprepossessing town of Chindo. I wanted to find Mr Park Byung-chun, who is one of the Saesumodang shamans by inheritance and an initiate of the Chindo *Ssikkimkut*. Mr Park was anxious to make it clear to me that they consider their beliefs to be folk ancestor religion, the worship of the spirits of their ancestors, the origins of which he feels are lost in history. He agreed that I could watch the ceremony, and suggested that I might like to go to the beach to see them bless the spirits of those who had died at sea.

The original ceremony is very long and can last all night, but there is a shortened version which has grown up in the last few years as a result of what is known as the Cultural Asset System – the Chindo *Ssikkimkut* was declared an Important Intangible Cultural Property on 7 November 1980. The abbreviated form is just a performance, rather than a religious ceremony, and can be shown in a concert hall or wherever. Although I was saddened to feel that there had been an attempt to ossify the ceremony, I decided I was being unjust. The full religious ceremony obviously still means a great deal to the local population, and it does no harm for the rest of the nation and visitors to be able to see a short version of this ancient ritual.

Down on the beach, which was fringed by pine trees, we were joined by three musicians and two *mudang* (shamans). I discovered that one of the musicians was going to play the *changgo,* another a *kayagum* and the third man a bamboo oboe called a *piri* – but he also had a gong. He turned out to be the leader. It was explained to me that the word *ssikim* means 'to wash' – so this is a washing ceremony.

There are six parts to the *Ssikkimkut,* I was told, starting with the *Samhyeon* in which members of the family of the deceased for whom the *kut* is being made offer wine in the sacred area. This is an instrumental interlude, the music of which is repeated between the parts of the rest of the ceremony. The *mudang* then performs the *Chohonjiak,* which is a song invoking the presence of the spirits and inviting them to cleanse their souls. This is followed by *Sonnimkut,* a question and answer session between the *mudang* and the musicians regarding the origins of Sonnim, the god of smallpox. There is then a *kut* honouring Chesok, one of the two tutelary gods of Buddhism who is responsible for providing life, children and wealth, and this invokes blessings for the living. Following the *Chesokkut* is the *Hon Ssikimkut,* in which the ill feelings of the dead are symbolically wiped away with a broom and purification is conducted using wormwood and perfumed water. The final part of the ceremony is the *Kil Takkum,* a ritual for purifying the path to heaven, which involves the use of a roll of white cotton fabric more than ten yards long which is stretched out in front of the musicians and the *mudang* and upon which the spirit box is placed.

I found it quite difficult to know where we had got to in the ceremony, although there were obvious changes of tempo, and I could see when we had reached certain points such as the question and answers and of course when the white cloth came out. The two *mudang* seemed to take it in turn to dance, although only one of them was the principal singer. I was surprised at how frequently the musicians sang as well. Considerable use was made of white paper cut into lengths which looked a bit like grass skirts. I discovered that this represented money, which made much more sense. When the ceremony was over, one of the audience smiled at me and told me that now the spirit was in a good place. I felt as comforted by that thought as she obviously did.

What I had just witnessed was a living expression of a faith whose roots are lost in the mists of time. Korea's cultural soul has not died or been subsumed into Western ways – it is still here, using the same form of expression as it has for thousands of years. Talking to my interpreter about what we had just seen, she mentioned that Christianity is the fastest-growing religion in Korea. The reason, she feels, is that the Christian Churches, as is their way, have seized upon the local beliefs and incorporated the ideology of shamanism into Christianity. I was much struck by her opinion and have since heard it repeated by many other Koreans.

Returning to Seoul, I saw the city with new eyes. It was night, and the thing I had noticed before was the huge number of neon signs. This is common in many cities, but what is different about Seoul is that many of the most prominent neon signs are the crosses on top of church spires. So this fast-growing religion, incorporates not only shamanism but modern neon as well. Korea is neither locked in the past nor has it abandoned it. It is a healthy, growing society which, despite having its culture suppressed for half a century, has found its roots again and is building upon them. Yes, much is being carefully conserved and is effectively dead; but shamanism, Buddhism and the country's folk music are still very much alive and of great importance to the people. Christianity is carefully cultivating a new order, but that too is rooted in the old.

As I struggled back on to my plane, clutching my *changgo,* I was profoundly grateful that I had had the opportunity to look beyond the concrete jungle of the capital to find the beautiful countryside with its graceful old buildings, charming people and living traditions. So many visitors to foreign countries never get beyond the airport and a luxury hotel, and I felt privileged to have seen so much and to have been made so welcome everywhere I went. The international language of music had stood me in good stead once again, and I left with the warm knowledge that I had made some new friends and learned something of their culture, and particularly their music, which would greatly enrich my own life.

MOROCCO
Juliet Stevenson

'I was already a nomad as a young girl, when I used to daydream as I gazed at the enticing white road leading off, under a more brilliant sun it seemed to me, into the delicious unknown.... For me it seems that by advancing into unknown territories, I enter into my life.' These words were written at the end of the last century by the writer Isabelle Eberhardt, who, though born a Russian and brought up in exile in Geneva, escaped from Europe in her late teens to travel through North Africa in search of another identity.

In recent years much has been written about the phenomenon of the nineteenth-century woman traveller – that extraordinary breed of intrepid individualists who upped and left provincial and domestic lives to explore what an imperialistic Europe saw as 'uncharted' territory on the continents of Africa, Asia and the Americas. But Isabelle Eberhardt was different. Unlike the others, who travelled with financial backing, took all the baggage of their culture with them, and indeed were often motivated by missionary zeal, she went alone with no resources, rejecting the certainties of nineteenth-century Europe. Driven by a passion for the Arab world, she learned its language, converted to Islam and invented for herself a new persona – Si Mahmoud, a young male scholar from Tunisia.

Isabelle was an adventuress in the wildest sense, travelling without safety nets through Algeria and Morocco, purging her past, embracing what she found, and in perpetual

Heavily veiled and robed, women go about their daily tasks in Tamgroute.

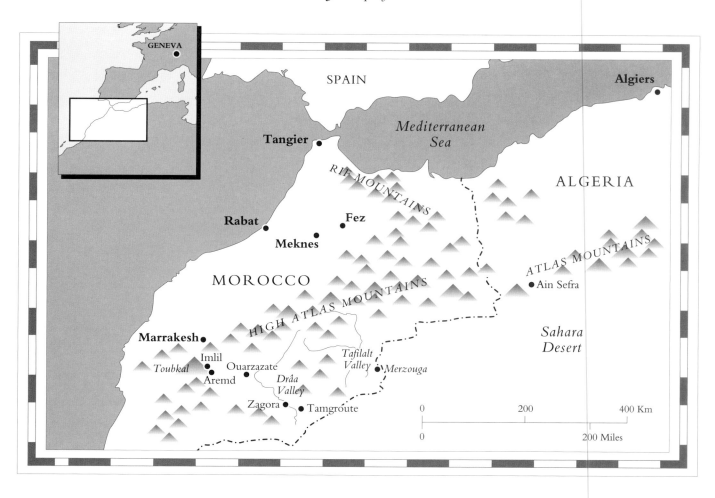

pursuit of a new beginning. Her life lent itself to posthumous legend-making, and since her early death in 1904 at the age of twenty-seven, when she drowned in a flash flood in the Sahara, she has become something of a cult figure – whether seen as a prototype feminist, the first hippie, a wildly romantic orientalist, or a promiscuous and self-destructive libertine. In any one of these interpretations there may be partial truths, but no complete ones. What is concrete, however, is the body of her writing – a novel, copious articles, letters and essays, an intimate journal and a large number of short stories inspired both by her own experience of desert life and by what she drew from the rich oral tradition of the people with whom she lived and travelled.

My journey was an attempt to discover her – not literally to follow in her footsteps, but to seek out her traces. As though she were a character I was going to play, I wanted to look for clues about her, to understand a little better who she was. I wanted to get behind the myth and the enigma that her paradoxical life has left in its wake. I had made such trips before when researching roles for theatre or film (though not with film crews in attendance, and without the need to supply a 'product' at the end of the expedition) and I knew it was unlikely that this journey would provide conclusive answers. It's more a form of imaginative trail-sniffing, in which the exploration of character in some way parallels the exploration of a landscape – you travel subjectively, bringing your own frame to what you see and find; you hunt around for clues and clarifications, while always knowing that there will be few, if any, objective truths. And at the heart of this particular journey, there was an irony – how do you seek out the identity of someone who was herself in quest of one, who re-created and redefined herself as she went further into the unknown?

I went first to Geneva, Isabelle's birthplace and the city which served as a springboard for her escapades. Born the illegitimate daughter of an aristocratic Russian mother and an Armenian anarchist father, she was to write of her childhood here almost exclusively as miserable and suffocatingly narrow-minded. I wondered why. I had seen some old archive film footage of Geneva at the period when she was growing up there, from which I gleaned the impression of a stolid, industrial, perhaps rather complacently prosperous place. But it was also a democratic, independent city that offered refuge to countless political refugees and exiles from a turbulent Europe at the end of the last century – Isabelle's own family amongst them. Does it still possess this rather contradictory identity? What remains, a hundred years later, of the place she knew, that would throw up any clues as to why she shot out of it at the earliest opportunity?

I arrived on a damp, overcast and misty morning, the city lying shrouded in a shadow-less grey light. It seemed an appropriate source of melancholy for an adolescent girl who dreamed of the brilliance of a desert sun. On the face of it, you needn't look far in present day Geneva to have a sense of what a dissident spirit might have found to be stifling. It presents itself to the world as an affluent, conservative, hygienic city, preoccupied with commerce and the creation of wealth. Above the wide facades of the nineteenth-century buildings that frame the lake hang innumerable neon signs advertising banks, corporations and insurance companies. Wandering around the city centre, along its pristine streets and vaulted shopping malls, where countless luxury goods proclaim their indispensability, signs of opulence abound and poverty appears to be an outlaw. Time seems to be something of an obsession. Rolex, Omega and Tissot battle it out for your attention from a plethora of hoardings and shop windows – time as money, split-second accuracy a measure of efficiency and high status. A sense of systematic order prevails – an elaborate network of escalators, elevators and tramways take you effortlessly where you need to go, the pattern of their geometric lines echoed even in the paths of the city's central park. Here the founders of European Protestantism, carved in monumental stone, gaze out benignly over immaculate lawns and tidy borders. It struck me as a city confident in its own identity, in whose myriad spotless windows and gleaming surfaces its citizens see their own fixed images reflected back at themselves, reminding them, perhaps, at all times of who they are. I found myself wondering how you would survive here if you were not a traveller in straight lines and did not aspire to what the city seems to stand for – if you sought to dismantle who you had been told you were in order to discover other truths about yourself.

But I had also come to Geneva to meet a man who has been obsessed by Isabelle Eberhardt all his life. Claude Richox is a retired journalist and newspaper editor, who first read about Isabelle when he was only twelve and became haunted by the story of the cross-dressing young woman from Geneva and her travels in the Sahara. The connection was profound, and when he reached the age that she was when she left her home, he went to trace her footsteps in the desert regions of Algeria. He told me that, of all the women he had loved in his life (indicating that these were numerous), Isabelle retained first place in his heart: he sensed that in her travels she had been seeking something that he, too, had felt in quest of – a sort of 'spiritual peeling', as he put it. The experience of spending several years living among the Bedouin people and adopting their nomadic lifestyle had changed him profoundly – now, Claude told me, he can tell within a quarter of an hour of meeting someone for the first time whether or not they too have spent time in the desert.

We met in a small suburban park, all that remains now of the rambling grounds that once surrounded the house where Isabelle grew up. The Villa Neuve, then in an isolated hamlet, is now surrounded by suburban sprawl, the view of the Jura mountains obscured by vast gas cylinders. We spoke of her childhood here as the youngest of five children in a neurotic and dysfunctional family – her mother an ineffective invalid, her father a fervent anarchist whose utopian ideas about girls' education led him to dress her as a boy, teach her six languages and make her spend long hours in the grounds chopping wood, digging ponds and cultivating the tropical trees and plants that were one of his obsessions. She was by far the most able and resourceful of the children and dreamed from earliest youth of her escape, writing later in her journal of 'the first awakenings of my intelligence, when I used to admire the melancholy sunsets behind the high gloomy silhouette of the Jura, and try to fathom the huge mystery of my future'. Claude talked about her private isolation within the seclusion of her environment, from which Isabelle developed a sense of that being central to her identity which she later pursued to even greater lengths in the Algerian desert.

I returned to the centre of the place Isabelle rather colourfully described as 'this evil city, where I have suffered so much and have come close to perishing'. Her diary entries, it must be said, are highly mood-influenced. In other passages she describes with glee the times she had there, running around dressed as a boy sailor, making sexual liaisons at a precociously early age, and attending political meetings 'right under the noses of agents' – the family were almost certainly under observation by the secret police because of their involvement with anarchist organizations in the town. I wondered what remained of the Russian exile community, of which Isabelle was once a part, after a hundred years of inter-marriage and absorption. In the old Russian Orthodox church, three priests conducted an evening service for a congregation of two. Raised as an atheist, Isabelle was unlikely ever to have attended the place, but as I sat there listening, something occurred to me. Prior to his exile from Russia, her father had been an Orthodox priest before vehemently unfrocking himself – perhaps his rejection of the Church was a precursor to Isabelle's subsequent rejection of the entire community.

It was time to move on – I was impatient now to leave Geneva. To explore a city merely in the light of how it had forced her out was of limited interest, and destined to do an injustice to the place. Departing, we drove round Lake Geneva once again, its unruffled surface dark and glassy. It struck me then how significant a part water came to play in the life of Isabelle Eberhardt – born by this lake, a river running through the gardens of the Villa Neuve, separated from the land of her aspirations by the straits she came to cross many times, drowned before the age of thirty. Water, too, is a central symbol in the Islamic creed that was the driving force behind her departure from the shores of Europe.

Isabelle first arrived in North Africa in May 1897, aged twenty. On the day she set out by boat from Marseilles, she wrote in her journal: 'The weather is grey and stormy and dark. Where am I going? Where destiny is taking me!' Subsequently, poverty and banishment by the French colonial authorities would oblige her to make the journey across the Mediterranean several times. When arriving in Algiers from Europe she once wrote with exhilaration, that she 'had that feeling of well-being, of rejuvenation I always get when reaching the blessed coast of my African fatherland'. At other times, however, she wrote with loathing of Algiers. I wondered where the root of this schizophrenia lay. An outbreak of violent fundamentalist activity had rendered Algeria out of bounds to us during the setting up of this journey, so I went instead to Tangier to look for the answer.

Arriving there, I found myself sharing her exhilaration. Though only twelve miles from Europe, with Spain clearly visible across the straits, you feel straightaway that you've stepped into a completely different culture, the threshold of unknown territory. You step off the boat to be sensually bombarded – Tangier is a marketplace and it begins at the port, which teems with traders, hustlers, buyers and sellers. Fresh from the sedentary pace of Geneva, the rhythm of the streets here struck me as hectic and relentless, some mad tarantella danced to the music of survival. As you come through the harbour gates, though, the past appears as a visible reality, immediately evident. A long facade of nineteenth-century French architecture fronts a square that reverberates with cries and car horns, the air thick with the smell of diesel. In Isabelle's time, this was a part of town out of bounds to Arabs, a promenade filled with the muslin and parasols of the colonial bourgeoisie, who built it in the pattern of a French provincial town. Now, fading and tatty, it has been happily recolonized by the Moroccans: wrought iron balconies are draped with rugs and laundry, and televisions blare from the doorways of cafés.

The first thing Isabelle would do on arrival was to shed her European identity like a snake's skin and create her Arab persona of Si Mahmoud. Dressing in baggy trousers, slippers, waistcoat, burnous and fez, she would slip off into the *medina*, the old Arab quarter of the town. She spent much of her time here in cafés, lounging on rugs before the doorway as was the custom, smoking the kif plant to which she became addicted, enjoying the

Overleaf: Entrance to the labyrinthine medina *in Tangier,*
where Isabelle Eberhardt easily assumed a new, Arab identity.

161

languor of male companionship and conversation. I, too, headed swiftly for the *medina,* up the winding road that hugs the cliff towards the clinging throng of flat-roofed, whitewashed houses, bound by the kasbah wall, that overlook the lower town. Walking through the maze of narrow, shaded alleyways, through tiny sunlit squares and up twisting flights of steps, it was not hard to understand why Isabelle felt the need to submerge so completely in order to feel a part of it. I became aware of a paradox. On the one hand, life appears to be lived out to the full in public; in these communal spaces the activities of daily life are being pursued palpably and visibly around you – water drawn from taps and wells; children washed; food cooked, sold and consumed; clothing and artefacts made, traded, carried, put to use. The tasks of existence are evident and tangible to the outsider. But on the other hand you have the sense of being utterly locked out – the architecture of the houses is such that you have absolutely no idea what's going on inside them, behind the blind windows and dark doorways, beyond the dead-end passageways. Somehow it resembles the landscape of a dream, labyrinthine and alien, where the more you walk the less you feel you'll ever gain control of your direction. Isabelle loved the secretiveness of this architecture, boxes within boxes, protecting their privacy through a subtle system of exits and entrances, reflecting perhaps what she admired about the Arab character – proud, impenetrable and discreet.

I realized that the Arab world would remain impenetrable unless, like her, I had the capacity to submerge into it. And necessary, too, to be male. Though women are in evidence, going purposefully about their business, the town seems to belong to the men. Segregation of the sexes seems to be an unerring rule – no mingling here, and even children seem to stick to their respective genders. To pass any one of the countless cafés is to glimpse a sea of men's faces, wreathed in cigarette smoke, gazing at the television screen upon the wall, glasses of mint tea cooling on the table tops. If, as Isabelle did, you wanted to socialize or find a lover, eat or gather stories, it would be inconceivable to do so as a woman, and much more so if you had come, like her, as a writer in search of material and inspiration. Paul Bowles, who has lived here for sixty years and through his writing has done much to shape our perception of Tangier, talks of this: 'Attempts undertaken to make a place accessible to the visitor are just so many barricades in the way of the writer … and if he manages to make contact with the place it will be in spite of them rather than thanks to them.… It takes an act of the imagination even to begin to connect.'

Tangier has for centuries been shaped by its identity as a place to be visited and passed through, a focal point for foreigners in search of a quick fix of exoticism, who stay only as long as appetite dictates and then return. But what of its more permanent residents, those

Opposite: In the medina *much of life goes on outdoors. Children play in the street and enjoy showing off for visitors.*

Overleaf: In the shade of the Anglican church of St Andrew, a chicken seller plies his trade.

for whom, like Isabelle or Paul Bowles, the attraction that first drew them to North Africa became compulsive, even a way of life?

Further up the town, surrounded by the crowded, clamorous streets that border the principal market square, lies the Anglican church of St Andrew, for a century the place of worship for the English-speaking community. It's an oddity, reflecting the hybrid nature of Tangier – the church delicately engraved with Moorish decoration, the churchyard as dappled, cool and verdant as any you might find in a Hampshire village. I dropped in out of idle curiosity, really, to have a peek at those who came here and, for whatever reason, stayed to bed themselves in, the living and the dead.

As I walked up the tree-lined path, a figure shot out of the church to greet me – Mustapha, a native of Tangier dressed in djellabah and burnous, but whose smattering of eccentric English was spoken in the tones of a Surrey vicar's wife welcoming her guests to a garden party. He told me, with radiant enthusiasm, that he had been the guardian here for thirty years, ringing the bell, changing candles, flower-arranging and tending graves. He has seen the English community, once pretty sizeable, dwindle to a mere 150, many of whom have already booked their burial plot up here; as we talked, a handful of elderly expatriates, tweed-suited in spite of the heat, strolled up the path to Matins.

Mustapha led me through the graveyard where the headstones said it all – generations of Mildreds and Elizas, Huberts and Harrys, who came for reasons military or missionary, lived out their lives here much in the manner of the old country, and died early deaths from malaria under an African sun. One grave, though, stood out from the rest – that of Walter Harris, who was *The Times* correspondent in Morocco during the last decades of the nineteenth century and the first three of this. Like Eberhardt, he dressed as an Arab and travelled deep into the country, submerging himself into its culture, becoming a passionate and brilliant chronicler of the period of the last sultans through to the establishment of the French and Spanish Protectorates. His grave, inscribed in Arabic and English, records his death in 1933.

'Same me!' cried Mustapha with delight.

'What do you mean, exactly?' I asked, perplexed. Then, with a flash, 'Oh! You were *born* in 1933?'

'Yes,' he beamed. 'It's lovely. Very nice.'

I had so enjoyed meeting this most courteous and joyous man that when I left I kissed him on both cheeks.

'Goodness!' said a member of the congregation who observed it. 'How very brave.'

I thought it might be time to leave Tangier. The excitement I had felt in its 'otherness' on arrival was starting to pall. You begin to sense a place with a shifting and uneasy identity. For decades a city of refuge and exile, beyond governmental discipline, a warehouse of forbidden fruits for the adventuring visitor, perhaps it has so shaped itself to serve the needs and expectations of all those passing through that it no longer quite knows who or what it is. Characterized by transience, it seemed to me less of a destination than a gateway through which to glimpse what lies beyond. Perhaps in my own restless impulse to move deeper into the country lay the clue to Isabelle's schizophrenic response to Algiers where, after her initial joy at being on African soil again had worn off, she wrote in her journal:

> The true African landscape is not to be found in any of the large cities.... Vast space and emptiness, a blinding light, are what makes a landscape African! The architecture of Algiers boasts none of those traits ... the uninitiated European thinks those men in dirty burnouses over tattered European clothes and those Moorish women are all part of the local colour. But this is precisely what is so un-Arabic about Algiers, for it is contrary to Arab custom.... Oh, how evil civilization is! Why was it ever brought over here?

Sharing her impatience to experience a more authentic African landscape, I boarded a train for Fez. Almost immediately I was brought up short by my own preconceptions. Throughout the four-hour ride south across the north-west plain and skirting the Rif mountains, the view remained relentlessly familiar – these could almost have been the lowland pastures of Isabelle's Switzerland. So what was I expecting to see? And what did she mean by a 'true Arab landscape'? *Her* expectations were first fuelled by the orientalist movement in Europe that attended on late nineteenth-century colonialism; *mine* were fed by the similar influences of late twentieth-century tourism. Were we not both guilty of bringing some mythic concept of the Arab world to our travels? We are inclined to reject what we find if it doesn't seem to fit, describing it as 'unreal' or 'degenerated'. But the tattooed face of the Berber woman sitting next to me on the train was a reminder that in this country many worlds coexist, and always have done.

It wasn't until this century that Morocco emerged as a nationstate. Prior to this, it was a sort of patchwork of tribes, whose shifting alliances and spasmodic bids for power defined both the government and its extent. With the odd exception, the ruling Arab sultans only ever controlled the northern plains and ports and the areas around the imperial capitals of Fez, Marrakesh, Meknes and Rabat. These were known as 'the lands of the governed'. The rest – the mountain ranges of the Rif and Atlas and the desert south – were known as 'the lands of the dissidents', and were populated by Berbers, the pre-Arab inhabitants, who seldom recognized anything more than local tribal authority, and still don't to a large extent. The only element that unifies this patchwork is Islam. Perhaps it was appropriate, then, that my next stopping-off point would be Fez, historically one of the holiest cities of the Islamic world.

The French called the city *'Fez la Mystérieuse',* and whatever you deem mystery to mean, it is not hard at first sight to see why. Wrapped tightly round by an ancient wall, still

Rooftops in Fez, one of Islam's holy cities.

virtually impenetrable by car, Fez seems reluctant to unrobe itself to the visitor. Even viewed from above, it is hard to get a sense of its internal shape as it lies shrouded under an emerald-green roofscape, punctuated only by the minarets of its 320-odd mosques. The most complete medieval city of the Arab world, Fez appears to have rejected European influence and infiltration as whole-heartedly as Tangier has embraced it.

Plunging for the first time into its arterial network of tiny streets, threaded with innumerable passages and alleyways like so many cauterized capillaries, I felt like Alice, outsized and out of time. Apart from the electric light bulb, there is nothing to indicate the arrival of the nineteenth, let alone the twentieth century. The ways are lined with diminutive workshops, in whose dark recesses the raw materials of the land are fashioned into artefacts by methods quite unaltered since medieval times. Craftsmen sharpen blades, melt and hammer brass and copper, tan and tool leather, spin and weave wool, stitch, embroider, bake and beat, using only what natural elements provide, and simple tools. Feet used as hands, teeth as fingertips, legs as pistons. These skills, though bone-achingly arduous, are practised with a deftness, sensuality even, that speak of centuries of continuity. The air, alive with smoke and spark, resonates with the sound of pounding metal as in some Renaissance town where a new church spire is being built.

Walking through the *medina* here came as a relief after Tangier – the concentration on these activities, the indifference to the visitor, the sense of the past alive in the present made me feel, paradoxically, less shut out. As a stranger, getting lost seemed a feature of the territory – as with the circuitous nature of Arab conversation, there are fifty possible ways to get from A to B. I came to a residential area where towering walls on either side permits only a sliver of sky to slip between, and all intrusive sound seems consumed into the stone. The *medina* is a place of co-existing extremes – of darkness and light, noise and silence, permanence and decay, revelation and concealment. Moving along the dense and sunless alleyways, where two mules constitute a traffic jam, it is impossible to guess at the expansive, luminous spaces that lie behind the walls. But I had met up with a guide. Abdellatif El Hajami is an architect responsible for restoring many of the city's threatened Islamic buildings, and he led me to the site of one of his projects, the fourteenth-century *medressa* of Bou Inania.

There are several *medressas* in Fez, of which this one is apparently the jewel, and constitutes one of the most important religious buildings in the city. The word *medressa* means 'place of study', and they were built as student colleges and halls of residence, comprising dormitories, study halls and mosque. We turned out of a cramped and hectic street into a dark, domed entrance chamber, climbed a flight of steps and passed through a low wooden door, and then suddenly I found myself standing in a huge, light-drenched courtyard of breath-stopping beauty. Marble-floored, it is flanked by four walls every inch of which are covered with elaborate decoration. White ceramic tiles, laced with rich elemental colours, ornament the walls from ground to human height. Above the tiles, a deep band of intricately carved cedarwood rises to the stuccoed plaster of the higher storey. Looking up,

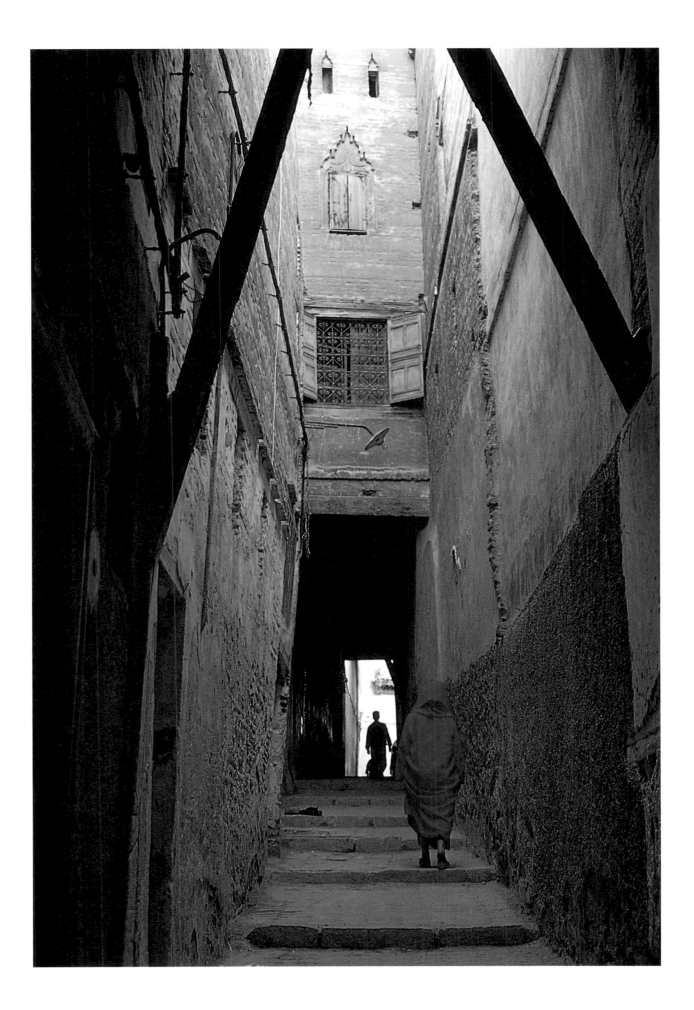

Two men pass the time in conversation as they wait for alms outside a mosque in Fez.

Opposite: A fez-wearing metalworker hammers his copper pots to shape in one of the many passages of the medina.

Previous page: A quiet, shady alley in the medina *in Fez.*

a scallop-edge of jade-green roof tiles frames a wide expanse of sky. The universe, Abdellatif told me, is always a participating element in Islamic architecture – divine creation and human creation blending to provide a context for contemplation. Similarly, the architectural design – calligraphic in the wood, geometric in the tiles and stucco – does not exist as ornament for its own sake, but as a setting in which the Muslim at prayer is reminded always of his human-ness. The intricacy of pattern and line, the diversity of colour, make no single aesthetic statement that might distract the worshipper's attention from God, but if his concentration wavers or is overwhelmed his eye can come to rest on the living movement of the pattern, a balanced and blended backdrop of human height and scale. This is art not as mere object, but inter-active, serving always to place the relationship to God in context.

The reflection of Islamic philosophy in its architectural form is evident in many ways. In the centre of the courtyard, a wide, round pool was continually refilled with running water – for symbolic or practical purposes? I wondered. As the midday call to prayer resounded, the question was more or less answered – a straggle of men came through the gate and went immediately to wash there. Abdellatif explained that in Islam water is the active symbol of purification, and each must cleanse himself before entering the mosque. There is a precise order in which parts of the body are washed, and each three times. Since prayer takes place five times a day, the practising Muslim is thus kept in frequent contact with this element of divine creation. Water as the symbol of life runs through the Koran as a recurrent theme, and its presence is central in the construction of both domestic and religious buildings.

I remembered the pleasure that Isabelle Eberhardt took in the ritualized disciplines of Islam, finding relief from her restless complexities in the simplicity and repetition of these practices. In one diary entry she writes: 'To be healthy in body, pure of all stains after bathing in clear water, to be simple and to believe, never to have doubted, never to have battled against oneself ... that is peace, that is Muslim happiness, and who knows, perhaps it is also wisdom.' It would have suited her well, too, that Islam seems to be the most adaptable and portable of religions – Abdellatif told me that if, for example, you are somewhere where water is inaccessible, you can perform the purification with sand or even, failing that, with stone. And if you have no bricks with which to build a mosque, you can make it with wood, or clay, or even goat hide. Failing all else, all you really need is a pair of knees, and indeed throughout the journey I often saw men stopping where they stood in street or field, mid-activity, to go down on all fours at prayer times. Wherever Islam has arrived in the world to take a hold, it has sought not to impose upon local customs and ways of life but

The medieval medressas *of Fez are part mosque, part seminary.*
Their tranquil inner courtyards are embellished with a wealth
of geometrical and calligraphic carving that is typical of Islamic
decorative art.

to incorporate and absorb them. Walking around in Fez, it struck me that this continual blending of the practical with the spiritual was also reflected in the discretion of Islamic architecture. Unlike many Christian churches and cathedrals, often built to tower above or stand apart as symbols of authority and control, the mosques and medressas of Fez merge discreetly into the body of the city, suggesting a synthesis of religion with working life.

Isabelle Eberhardt's attraction to the Muslim faith was not, however, exclusively connected to the simplicity of its routine practices. Ever contradictory, hers was also a self-questioning and introverted nature. Perhaps as a reflection of this aspect of herself, she came to join a Sufi brotherhood, the Kadriya. There are several Sufi orders within Islam, of which the Kadriya was the first and oldest, founded to escape from certain of the more entrenched orthodoxies of 'mainstream' Islam as it had evolved, and to devote its members to a more purely mystical tradition. In essence, the goal of this tradition was to destroy the illusion of self and to pass into the consciousness of survival in God, consummated finally by making a good death. But by Isabelle's time, such brotherhoods had also come to function as social or political clubs, often feuding with each other. As a member of the Kadriya, very probably the first European woman ever to be initiated, Isabelle would also then have benefited from the hospitality and protection guaranteed to all members wherever they encountered each other – handy for a single woman travelling on her own and usually penniless. Her writings, however, contain very little about the workings of this order, perhaps because the mysteries of induction were traditionally secret. It was one of the facets of her life by which I felt most daunted. To discover more I went to observe a present-day gathering of the Kadriya in Fez.

A lot of complicated negotiation was necessary to arrange this visit, and there had been much uncertainty and confusion as to whether it was on or off. In the event I was allowed only a few minutes to observe, standing well behind the boundary line in the area allotted to non-members. The ceremony took place in a smallish room at the top of a dark staircase, off a poky little street that had yielded us no sign of the Kadriya's existence. A group of about a dozen men, in white hooded robes, sat in a semi-circle, chanting repetitively, their cadences undulating within a narrow tonal range. The content of their chant I could not deduce, but from time to time each drew his hands down from his face towards his chest, symbolic (I was later told) of the desire to bring the words into his heart. There were women present, but they sat apart, chatting occasionally and seem-ingly rather unconnected to events. It was easy to see why Isabelle could not have played an active role in the Kadriya without her male disguise, but impossible to glean any further understanding.

After the ceremony I waited in the street below for the sheikh, with whom an inter-view has been arranged. It was to be a long wait. Sounds of fierce argument erupted in the room above, and one by one the men emerged, looking heated and disgruntled. Eventually the sheikh himself descended, seeming anxious and keen to lead us off to some more tranquil, private place. It transpired that we had unwittingly sparked off a row of some proportions between the sheikh and various members of his family – about what, exactly, it was impossible to clarify, but it appeared to be a political affair. Either they resented the fact that he had appointed himself spokesman for the Kadriya without their consultation, or felt that this was their prerogative, or perhaps that he should not agree to talk to us at all. Whatever the truth of the matter, it left the sheikh clearly nervous throughout the interview that followed. He continually looked about as though in fear of being overlooked, and responded to my questions with the most monosyllabic and bland of answers. I had hoped to draw him out on many things, both spiritual and cultural – the various stages to contemplation, the Sufi's relationship to death, how the brotherhood had evolved since Isabelle's time, how it differed from other comparable Sufi sects, and so on, but the sheikh's responses were somehow whitewashed and unyielding, rather in the manner of some Islamic Tourist board. Whether this was to do with our mishandling of affairs, whereby in our naivety we had exposed him to all manner of resentments and power struggles, or whether it was in itself a measure of how much of its mystical tradition the Kadriya had lost, was not yet possible to know. Perhaps both.

But as so often when you are travelling, the very problems and frustrations you encounter are the source of realization, of an inch more understanding. Reflecting later on the incident, it struck me that the whole mission of this journey was conceived around an irony – we had come from Europe with our schedules and our urgency, with our desire for accessible answers and digestible information, to a country and a culture where the relationship to time is utterly different, where definitions of what is true are infinitely subjective and multi-layered, and may take lifetimes to get near. And it was for this that Isabelle herself had come and in rejection of nearly everything we stood for that she had left the shores of Europe.

But given all the givens it was time to leave Fez and move on, without yet understanding very much of what I'd seen.

Happily, though, I had met Latifa Lagzaoui, an anthropologist specializing in the changing role of women and religion in Morocco. She agreed to join me for part of the long bus ride to our next destination – Marrakesh. And I hoped that *en route* she would be able to demystify certain aspects of Sufism for me, or at least throw a beam of light on what its significance may have been for Isabelle. She was, after all, the first European woman ever to be initiated into a Sufi brotherhood, and I asked Latifa if the Kadriya's apparent acceptance of her was as surprising as it seems.

She told me that Sufism treats women more equally than does orthodox Islam, because of its focus on the private relationship between the individual and God. Eschewing intermediaries and hierarchical structures, its central ideal is mystical – the quest for union with God through the destruction of the illusion of self. Thus gender becomes, in theory, irrelevant and, therefore, less of a focus for discrimination. Latifa spoke of the extent to which Sufism emphasizes personal experience rather than concern itself with an individual's culture or gender.

For similar reasons, Sufism has historically laid great emphasis on the importance of rejecting materialism and, indeed, all forms of worldliness. Money, goods, and material aspirations are viewed as further impediments to the Sufi goal of passing into consciousness of God and of making a 'good death'. I wanted to know more about the relationship to death, since Isabelle was very drawn to the idea of suffering, even seeking it out, and was often preoccupied with notions of death. Did this, I wondered, find some reflection in Sufism? Latifa told me that 'it's not so much Sufism, it's Islam in general … which sees death as a gift from God.' The road towards death, and being reunited with God, may be full of pain and suffering, but since it is the journey towards being united with Allah, you must bear and even enjoy it. To suffer is to be tested in some way, and in the endurance of the test there may be sweetness, even a kind of ecstasy. This, apparently, is something that classical Sufism takes from Islam, and which corresponds, I could see, to how Isabelle often wrote of her journey through life.

In fact, after several hours of talking with Latifa on the bus, several choices of Isabelle's were beginning to make sense. I was reminded suddenly of those characters in Chekhov's plays – direct contemporaries of Isabelle's – who are defined by their fatalistic attitudes towards their own hardships and defeats. In Arabic, Islam means, literally, 'submission'. Maybe in Isabelle's becoming a Muslim that Russian tendency towards the resignation of hope found some reflection. Her poverty and her distaste for worldly possessions would also have found their echo in Islam. Even the fact that she was raised as an anarchist was beginning to cohere. Rejection of political structures and institutions and focus on individual action find a spiritual echo in Sufism, which also emphasizes the personal and is defined by its rejection of orthodoxy.

But despite her attraction to Islam's fatalistic heart, Isabelle never stayed for long in a state of resignation. Her desire to repress her aspirations, drives and hopes was not more powerful than their capacity to erupt again. The most contradictory and restless spirit, she had also a compulsion to live life right on the edge, and her sensual and physical appetites were voracious motivating forces behind many of her actions.

To arrive in Marrakesh is to feel immediately that these drives of hers would have impelled her there. A kind of unacknowledged magnet pulls you to its central square – the Djemaa el Fna, variously translated as the Place of Infinity or the Square of the Dead. Until the 1950s this was the arena in which ghoulishly elaborate public beheadings took place – today it is ferociously alive, a kind of theatre of celebration and desperation where spectacle and pageant are underpinned by a furious need to survive. Anything and everything is up for sale here – unidentifiable potions and cures for the sick from Atlas mountain herbs to grated iguana skin, broken teeth and old dentures, Koranic literature, imitation Reeboks, oranges, rubber tyres – you name it, nothing is too old or worn or unworkable to have a price. Innumerable skills are also on display: snake charmers, scribes, fortune tellers, jugglers, child acrobats, drag acts, musicians and dancers all compete for a yard of space and the visitor's attention and cash. As night comes on, the square's activities intensify –

numerous little cafés are erected, fires lit, and the senses are bombarded with the smells and sounds of food, steaming, sizzling, smoking. The month of Ramadan had just begun when we arrived – after the evening call to prayer announced the end of fasting for the day, an orgy of eating, drinking and smoking erupted. Palates that had tasted nothing since first light (Islamic law forbids even the swallowing of your own saliva during daylight hours) were released from their discomfort, and a wild exuberance was unleased as though by a starting gun.

To film here turned out to be nigh on impossible – to attempt to move around the place, quietly and mechanically recording examples of its pageantry, proved a farcical exercise. For we ourselves became, within an instant, the greatest pageant of the lot, ringed by a fascinated crowd who clustered round the camera and saw no need to respond to appeals for privacy and observer status on our part. As frustrations grew and tempers strained amongst the crew, who valiantly attempted to fulfil their brief, I thought again of how it is that obstacles in the path of tourists are often their best guides to a greater understanding of an unknown culture. Tourists often speak with rage of being 'hassled' in Morocco (and nowhere more than in the Djemaa el Fna) and of how neither pleading, screaming nor negotiating can deter the determined would-be guide or trader from sticking to their sides. But the 'problem' is compounded by what we bring from our own culture – at home, there is an unspoken consensus that the individual has a right to privacy in public. There is a radius of space around the body which is seldom entered by a stranger, except on rush-hour trains, and even here we manage to retain a silent separateness despite the bodies pressed against us. In England, we share a collective notion of 'own business' to be minded. In Morocco, a different cultural consensus exists – that if you are in public, then in essence you're up for grabs, and the concept of privacy is reserved exclusively for inside the home. How could it be otherwise in a country where so many live from day to day, surviving on their wits or their capacity to bargain and persuade, to exploit the opportunity of the moment? In Marrakesh, there are few certainties or securities for the vast majority who daily ply their trade there, and nowhere else in Morocco do you have a stronger sense of life lived in the raw, on the edge. This was a reality that Isabelle knew well: 'No-one has ever lived more from day to day and by chance than I have. And it is very much the events themselves, inexorably linked to one another, which have brought me to where I am and absolutely not me who has created them.'

Perhaps it was appropriate, then, that while in Marrakesh we ourselves were thrown up against the vagaries of chance. So far, an unbroken stretch of perfect, cloudless weather had blessed our journey, allowing filming schedules to be met more or less as planned. The first morning in Marrakesh, however, we awoke to lowering skies and heavy rain. What to do? Try to shoot it as it was, streets dripping and half empty? Sit it out until the sun returned? Move on and come back later? Anxious faces gazed up at the indifferent sky, scouring it for an answer. Finally a rather British decision was made to consult the local meteorological office for advice on which to make an informed decision. An urgent fax

*At the corner of the Djemaa el Fna in Marrakesh where the
cloth dyers ply their trade.*

*Overleaf: A crowd gathers in the Djemaa el Fna to watch
street entertainers perform.*

was sent, and the reply awaited. None came. A series of phone calls rang unanswered in an office somewhere. At last, after a long day of inactivity and mounting panic, someone was sent round to check the place out in person. The weather bureau was found to be unmanned, the urgent fax lying neglected on the desk – the weather man, perhaps either depressed or overjoyed by the unusual downpour, had taken the day off. Another example of the confounding nature of bureaucracy in this country, and another illustration of how, when encountering a problem, we ended up face to face with the impotence of our own systems of dealing with it.

I didn't care. I was impatient to get out of cities and into the more uncharted territory of the south. Cities were associated with unhappiness for Isabelle Eberhardt. She often felt oppressed and constrained by urban bureaucracies and administrative processes, by homogeneity and materialistic preoccupations. Ever viewed with acute suspicion by the colonial authorities centred there, Isabelle was often called to order by them and threatened with arrest and banishment. It was an attitude guaranteed, of course, to increase her ambivalence towards the European presence in North Africa and to strengthen her sense of identification with the Arabs who opposed it. Essentially nomadic by instinct, the problems she faced in the colonized cities spurred her to keep moving: 'The fundamental need of my nature is variety of scenery ... great difficulties and crises of despair recharge my energy and calm my nerves.... Monotony and mediocrity of settings and atmospheres, these are the enemies.'

I, too, had begun to feel that so far we had dwelt on that which pushed her, and was eager to experience now the pull, the draw of what lay beyond. Marrakesh, in any case, has that effect. Situated as it is just thirty-odd miles from the northern flanks of the High Atlas, the city is framed by the snowy crests of those mountains from every point inside it. On days when they are invisible, the place seems incomplete. As though the builders of the city saw each roof and terrace, spire and roadway in relation to the chain of glistening peaks beyond, the eye is continually encouraged to rise up towards the ramparts that encircle the old town and come to rest upon the mountains. In addition to this lure, I felt that there were few traces in Marrakesh of anything that would have held Isabelle for very long. If, to the visitor, Fez had been a courteous refusal, Marrakesh came as an unconditional embrace, which while meeting certain of her appetites, perhaps, would have compelled her to escape into a calmer, simpler landscape, further removed from the marketplace.

Up, then, into the High Atlas, climbing the giant spine of the country that divides the northern plains from the desert south. Our immediate destination was the village of Aremd, which sits about 5900 feet (1800 metres) up at the foot of the highest peak, Djebel Toubkal – 'the mountain of mountains'. The drive was one of the most beautiful I have ever made. As soon as it begins to climb, the road follows a winding river valley, through scattered villages and hamlets that cluster on its rocky sides, their roofs and walls of dried-blood red almost indistinguishable from the colours of the earth around. Innumerable terraces hewn into the mountainside were thick with fruit trees heavy with blossom, and washed with the new green of young crops. A recent fall of snow had left the valley strewn with white, dazzlingly so under the bright sun of the morning's drive, and the air intoxicatingly cool and fresh.

We climbed as far as possible in Land Rovers, to the village of Imlil about 5500 feet (1700 metres) up, where the road gives way to track and must be tackled by foot – or, for the feeble, hoof. I hiked with our party for the first part of the climb, and then, taking shameless advantage of being six months pregnant, hitched a mule ride the rest of the way. Lulled by the animal's steady, swaying gait and basking in the heat of a Moroccan February sun, I thus found myself – for the first time in this country – out in the open, in a landscape uncloistered by walls and shadows.

This is the heartland of the Berber people, the oldest inhabitants of North Africa. When the French began their 'pacification' policy in the 1920s, the Atlas Berbers' way of life was essentially feudal, controlled by three great clans who struggled to hold out against French domination for nearly twenty years. Today, the Berber villages retain a large measure of independence – they are not generally taxed, the role of the state is minimal, and government is through a system of local caids. The people of these villages take great pride in their separateness and self-determination. No Arabic is spoken here, they retain their own three dialects, their particular form of stone or clay architecture, their unique form of Islam and their own cultural traditions.

Music and dance are a big feature, and tend to happen fairly spontaneously. If the men of the village are bored or feel the impulse, they call to the unmarried girls to join them; and if there's a consensus, festivities begin. The imperatives of documentary film-making, however, tend to forbid reliance on the spontaneous event (a fact with which I found myself uneasy on occasion) and this morning we were expected in the village of Aremd. Still, this did little to deter my sense of thrill as, approaching the village from the opposite flank of the valley and crossing the river bed to reach it, the distant sound of women singing filtered through the air, gaining power with proximity like some sirens' call. No sirens, though, the young girls who awaited our arrival. Dressed for the dance in a brilliant array of kaleidoscopic colours, in skirts and tunics bordered and belted with sequined braid and ribbon, and head-scarves of beaded lace, they sat on an outdoor terrace in a close circle, clapping their hands and singing in piercingly clear high voices. Around them on a low wall a group of men of all ages lounged and chatted. On our arrival they went immediately to fetch food, bringing out dish after dish of meat and couscous, plates of warm bread and pots of steaming mint tea.

After eating, we all descended to a field below, where the villagers laid out large and brilliant carpets on the crisp white snow and took their places for the dance. This was

Overleaf: After recent snow in the High Atlas, Juliet and the rest of the party have to go on foot or by mule where the track is not even passable to Land Rovers.

185

*The young unmarried girls of Aremd, unveiled and gorgeously
attired, sing and dance for the visitors.*

*Opposite: The Berber village of Aremd, high in the mountains.
Despite the former French colonization of Morocco, the Berbers
have always maintained a degree of independence and still preserve
their own language, culture and religion.*

structured round a wide circle, men on one side, women on the other – positions from which they rarely moved except when individuals from each group stepped forward to the centre of the ring to come together. To the accompaniment of half a dozen hand drums, the song began and then swelled up to the peaks above, a sort of call-and-response exchange that stayed within an octave's range, its cadences continually repeated. I was told that the essence of this musical dialogue was that the men called for God to help them, and the women replied that all would be well – but watching on the sidelines, it didn't seem to me to be all that was going on. Here, refreshingly, the girls all went unveiled, and with shaking shoulders and rotating hips seemed freer to communicate a sensuality never visible to visitors to traditional Arab communities.

Later, as the sun slipped over the mountains and shadows began to lengthen across the valley's stretch, we walked back up to the village again to gather on the terrace. Here, over more mint tea, the son of the head of the village, a young man called Lahcen Id Belaid, told me the story of its legendary origins.

The Belaid family were the first to settle there, and one of them – Lahcen's ancestor – kept a horse. During a religious festival he did not attend to this horse for three days, and so was surprised when, visiting the animal on the fourth day, he found it hot and sweating as though it had been freshly exercised. He was very puzzled by this and he decided to observe it closely. Now, at around the same time a strange dog had come to live in the village, and it had been taken in by the Belaid family and given shelter. Imagine the amazement of Lahcen's ancestor when, while keeping a secret watch that night over his stabled horse, he saw this dog slip into the stable and transform itself into a man, dressed in gown and turban and with a staff in one hand. Mounting the horse, the dog-man rode it out to a field above the village, where he proceeded to ride races with other equestrian spirits before returning at dawn to stable it again and transform himself back into his canine form.

For three nights the ancestor observed this, saying to himself: 'What is this creature? A human being or an evil spirit?' Then he thought of an idea. He prepared two plates of couscous, one with salt in it and one without, and laid them out for the dog to find on its next nightly excursion. Now human beings cannot bear to eat couscous without salt, whereas evil spirits have the same relationship to salt as vampires do to garlic – so in the dog's choice of dish would lie the answer. That night the dog returned and, after trying both, devoured the unsalted couscous with great relish. The ancestor confronted the strange creature, begging him in the name of God to state exactly what kind of being he was. 'I am the Lord of the Evil Spirits', came the answer, 'and my name is Sidi Charamouche. Look at me carefully and see the staff that I hold in my hand. Tomorrow you must go up the river and, wherever you find this staff lying on the ground, there you must build me a holy shrine, a marabout. Henceforward you will be in charge of it and take collections there, for many will come to the place to seek cures, above all the mentally sick who have been struck by evil spirits – here, they will be healed.'

So the next day the ancestor summoned the people of the village and told them all that he had heard and witnessed. Then they went upriver to the place where the staff lay and built a shrine there, as commanded. And, to this day, on 22 August every year, the mentally ill are brought from all over Morocco to the shrine. The Festival of Sidi Charamouche takes place there for three days, with feasting and prayer and making of sacrifices.

I was intrigued, in this story, by the seamless blend of Animistic and Islamic creed, the power of God and the power of the spirit-animal sharing comparable status, as it seemed. So the incoming religion derives its rituals and histories from the foundations of the one it seeks to over-rule. Absorption, rather than replacement. I was interested, too, by the ambiguous nature of the so-called evil spirit, which in the story initially employs foul means to achieve ends that work for the common good – this is, I gather, a feature found elsewhere among shamanic traditions. There is an abundance of such stories in Berber culture, through which their history is recounted as a blend of fact and legend, integrally woven. On the whole, Berber history is not written down and there is virtually no literature, so the oral tradition remains rich and diverse, still prevalent as a source of education, entertainment and identity.

Moving on and over the high pass to the southern slopes of the mountain range, we were to encounter further examples. We were heading for a rendezvous with another Berber community, this time a family of nomads belonging to the Ait Atta, the 'super-tribe' among the nomadic Berber tribes of the Atlas. It was another memorable journey. Descending these south-facing slopes towards the foothills, it is astonishing how quickly and dramatically the landscape changes, drying out and paring down, as though with every dozen miles or so the earth sheds another layer of skin. Alpine snows and pasturelands give way to craggy cliff and rock, where a profusion of minerals emerge on the cliff face as a palette of purples and reds, violets and indigos. Further down, this riot of colour is bleached away, subdued by drier tones of dun and burnt sienna as the influence of the desert begins to encroach. We turned off the main route south to head east along the Djebel Sarhro – this is the beginning of the Moroccan Sahara, a vast expanse of stone and scrub broken only by isolated outcrops of unyielding rock that loom, hieroglyphic, over the surrounding plain. As the land dropped down my adrenalin rose, sensing the pull of what lay beyond. Space began to open up, skies to widen, time to have less significance, to stretch....

Crossing a stark, exposed, dry plateau in the Sarhro range, we caught up with Ali Louche and his family and herds. The territories covered by the Ait Atta are wide and diverse, stretching from the snow-covered heights of the Atlas down to the Sahara, and from the Drâa valley to the west to the Tafilalt valley in the east. Traditionally, the pattern of their journeying is defined by grazing needs and trading posts – summer spent on the grasslands of the high peaks, winter on the edge of the desert. But Ali Louche, head of the family and a man of nearly seventy, feels too old to do that now, so he limits their travels to the lower slopes and plateaus of the range, staying sometimes up to three months in one place. His brother even owns land now, and farms it, so the family is divided between a

Ali Louche breaks camp with his dromedaries.
Traditionally these herdsmen spend the summers on the rich
grasslands of the mountainsides, and come down to the fringes
of the desert when the weather starts to deteriorate.

Opposite: Sara, Ali Louche's young wife, herding goats,
as her ancestors have done for centuries.

Bringing back firewood for the evening campfire.

settled and nomadic existence. When necessary he sells some of his goats in market towns along the route, buying grain and other staples in exchange.

We met them at the site of their previous night's encampment – Ali Louche, his second young wife Sara, their five-year-old son and baby daughter, and two cousins. (I was introduced to each male member of the family in turn, but never to his wife.) With impressive speed the camp was dismantled, folded, stowed away on paniered mules and dromedaries, and we set off, the men walking together with the larger animals, Sara always at a distance with the sprawling herd of goats, her small son at her side and her baby strapped in shawls to her back. We spent a day walking with the family – a luxurious amount of time within the schedule of a documentary film crew, an irony which resonated loudly in the company of people for whom time is measured at the pace of footsteps. But in searching through this country for traces of Isabelle Eberhardt, I felt that at last I had struck a nerve. She was an insatiable wanderer herself, through both choice and necessity. Her time in the south was spent largely in the company of nomadic people, as guides and companions, and they were the source of much of what she most felt akin to and eased by, often providing the material of her richest writing. In one short story, 'The Drama of Hours', she writes:

> To travel is not to think, but to see things in succession, with one's life sensed in the measure of space. The monotony of landscapes slowly unrolling soothes our cares, infuses us with lightness and quiet which the fevered traveller could never know on his full-speed excursions. At the unhurried pace of horses stunned by the heat, the smallest accidents of the journey preserve their startling beauty. These are not fretful predicaments; rather a calm and vital state of mind rules, which once belonged to all human races and is still preserved among us in the blood of nomads.

But the rhythms of this day had their own volatility; as dusk fell, a sense of sharpening need set in – to enclose the animals, set up camp and eat before all light had left the sky. We turned off, out of the shallow, dry river bed whose course we had been following along the plateau, and stopped at a crumbling, low, dry stone-walled enclosure, evidently a regular stopping-off point along their route. Here, once more with astonishing speed and deftness, the night's accommodation for both family and flocks was organized, Sara herding some straggling goats into a pen, the men unpacking paniers and setting up a heavy goatskin canopy with sticks and rocks, laying out rugs and gathering fragments of wood for the evening's fire.

Watching, I thought of another of Eberhardt's stories, autobiographical in tone, in which she writes:

> I have been penetrated by this idea: that one can never fall lower than oneself. When my heart has suffered, then it has begun to live. Many times on the paths of

my errant life, I asked myself where I was going, and I've come to understand, among the nomads, that I was climbing back to the sources of life; that I was accomplishing a voyage into the depths of my humanity. In contrast to so many subtle psychologists, I've discovered no new motivations, but I have recapitulated some primal sensations; through all the shabbiness of my adventures, the defining curve of my existence has been expanded.

I thought, then, of why it may have been that she so passionately identified with nomadic people – their self-reliance, their capacity to exist with only the barest of necessities, oblivious to the stimulus of artificial needs, their tough sensuality, all seem to lend them a virility and dignity which are the hallmark of their freedom. Perhaps among these people she sought to shake off old dependencies, to toughen her body and strengthen her spirit in order to realize the potential she felt in herself, a potential weakened by urban existence and its obsessive materialism. Standing there on the sidelines watching Ali Louche, footsore as I was and shivering with cold, I was conscious of my own enfeeblement by city life.

Over preparations for supper – a single loaf of bread, kneaded on a nearby rock and baked among the ashes of a fire made of palm fronds – the tireless Ali Louche began to tell a story. He has an enormous repertoire, apparently, but his favourite remains the history of his family's involvement in the battle of Bou Gafer, the site in 1933 of his clan's final defeat in their long-standing struggle against the French invaders. It is a story of technology versus ingenuity, the French with their planes and bombs, the Ait Atta merely with a handful of rifles and an intimate knowledge of the terrain. No surprises, then, as to the outcome – the encounter left the region strewn with dead, their livestock blown apart beside them, their crops and pastures devastated. To this day, Ali Louche told me, there remains a scattering of unexploded bombs embedded in the earth there. But he tells the story with great pride and relish, his features animated with accounts of Berber cunning – of rifles strapped to the under-bellies of camels, of families living for months on end in crevices of rock, of his own active participation as a child of eight or nine. 'I tell these stories to my children,' he concluded, 'and they will tell them to their own.' And, indeed, his silent little boy sat blinking in the firelight, rapt by an account he must have heard many times before.

It was to glean and gather stories such as these, above all other reasons, that Isabelle was motivated to travel in the south. Listening and absorbing, and then weaving the contents into her stories and vignettes of desert life, were perhaps her gift back to a people from whom she received boundless hospitality and help. The modernity and vigour of her writings on the subject must have offered a radically different perception of the people she chronicled, hitherto shrouded either in a fog of romanticized orientalism or demonized to serve the ends of colonizers.

It was, then, with a sharpened sense of her paradoxical nature that I headed further south next morning. We were entering now the flattening plains of the Sahara's edge, going ever deeper into the landscape by which Isabelle was most lured. Yet although she loved and identified fiercely with this area and with the people of the south, she came to work for General Lyautey, the French officer most responsible for colonizing North Africa, the man who was attempting to bring the colonized into line with French notions of 'civilization'. Her travels to these parts were thus driven partly by pragmatism. In return for payment from Lyautey she consented to a sort of mole-like mission – as a Sufi, she was able to gain access to *zaouias,* centres of religious and political authority which, in these desert regions, were the focus of resistance to French plans. Ever disguised as Si Mahmoud, the Tunisian boy scholar, once installed she was supposed to use her influence to encourage the compliance of the *zaouia* chiefs. In mitigation, it should be said that in the event she seldom fulfilled the brief, having little heart for it and even less political drive, and being easily seduced by her surroundings.

We were now heading for one such place, the *zaouia* of Tamgroute. Following the course of the river Drâa, its narrow silver ribbon trail the only visual relief amongst a landscape of monochrome baked earth, we passed through little but the occasional oasis town before reaching our destination. In the pattern of all such desert settlements, Tamgroute consists of a clutch of fortified kasbahs ringed with palms, and clusters round the building that lies at its core, the *zaouia. Zaouias* are to be found all over North Africa. Founded by the Sufi brotherhoods, they were usually built around the tomb of a *marabout* or holy man, and so constitute the symbolic spiritual heart of the town or village. Historically they were also major centres of social, political and economic networks, but now these secular powers are much reduced.

The *zaouia* in Tamgroute is one of the most prestigious in Morocco, combining many functions. Its rich library preserves a number of early Korans, written on gazelle hide and brought on camel-back from Mecca, which attract scholars from all over the Islamic world. The central open courtyard offers refuge to the physically and mentally ill, many of whom come to live here, cardboard city-style, in hope of a cure. Over the ubiquitous mint tea the current sheikh, a gentle and hospitable octogenarian, enlarged upon the workings of the place. He explained that there are no rituals of healing – hope, for the sick, resides in the belief that the aura of the *marabout* will help them out, though the *zaouia* does provide three simple meals a day and whatever alms it receives from visitors. Some people stay for many years; in fact, later on our driver found a friend amongst their midst, an ex-policeman from Casablanca who had left his wife and family twelve years before to live here in a box. Did he feel he was getting any better as a result of such sustained faith? 'A little,' he replied. Unlimited welcome is also offered to scholars of the Koran, who come here to pursue their studies in the library, and over all comers the sheikh, as the latest of a long line before him, presides as spiritual counsellor and figurehead.

Isabelle herself, often sick with malaria and syphilis, invariably destitute, made great use of *zaouia* hospitality. Here she was able to write profusely, finding rest and solace in seclusion and abstinence:

I am the guest of these men. I shall live in the silence of their house. Already they have brought me all the calm of their spirit and a shadow of peace has entered the recesses of my soul. Is this the life I came to find? Will all my longing finally be appeased, and for how long? I dream of a sleep that would be a death, from which one would emerge armed and strong, with a personality regenerated by forgetting.

Focussed by the tranquillity and timelessness of the place, between bouts of fever she wrote much of her best work in this environment. But, ever battling with contradictions, she was also tortured by sexual deprivation, and writes of this struggle as she imagines hearing outside the walls 'under the quiet stars, the ardent rutting … what agony! I almost want to bite into the warm earth. But the real ecstasy is above in the light of the stars, in the memory of eyes looked into … of hours lived, of hours so beautifully wasted.'

I often wondered, during this trip, whether her disguise was ever rumbled, and if so, how it was perceived and dealt with. It is hard to ascertain, but there is a clue during her *zaouia* stay. It seems that a doctor was summoned in secret to tend to the sheikh, who, uncharacteristically for a man in his position, appeared to be suffering from some venereal disease. It transpired that he was confident of the source – the young Tunisian scholar who was staying in the place. The matter seems to have been handled with discretion and without recrimination – and you have to deduce that, while aware of Isabelle's true identity and gender, the sheikh and others in the know were content to collude in her presentation of herself as a man, possibly because Arab politeness forbade otherwise, and because on occasion it offered a potential erotic encounter whose traces could be easily obscured.

Leaving the *zaouia,* I wandered out to look around the village: a little grid of shaded streets bordered by clean, mud-packed walls, whose density ensures that the houses tucked behind them remain protected from the scorching heat of day. The sense of a place un-altered by time was reaffirmed here. As with all desert villages human settlement is defined by water, and the business of irrigation is kept up with patience and persistence. Each family owns a small parcel of land, scored with tiny channels to conduct and distribute water, to ensure that every spare inch is exploited to grow wheat, barley and maize, creating little explosions of colour amidst the uniform baked earth around.

The size of each village is measured not in acreage, but in the number of palm trees that its oasis contains, of which each family will own a small number. Mule remains the mode of transport for both passenger and crop, and the unhurried pace of the animal seems to set the rhythm of the village – for here, time seems ample. Perhaps the struggle for existence against the rigours of geology and climate keeps the villagers always at first base, and therefore impervious to fluctuations other than those of weather and acts of God – no use here for rush and scramble, or for wrestling with the hours. A man will stand all

Previous pages: Palm trees at the oasis settlement of Tamgroute.

day in a field with his herd, or by the side of the road to sell a lump of mineral, or lounge and gaze at the horizon with no apparent objective. It was in such a place that Isabelle fantasized about living:

> I would like to settle there and make a home … a little mud house close to some date palms, a place to cultivate the odd vegetable in the oasis, a companion, a few small animals, a horse perhaps, and books as well. Fashion a soul for myself out there, an intelligence and a will … I have no doubt that my attraction to the Islamic faith would blossom magnificently out there.

Surely the fatalism at the heart of Muslim faith is linked, in part, to geography. This is a climate characterized by unpredictability, volatility, extremes – lakes appear and disappear within a week; drought or flood, violent storms of sand or rain may arrive at any time out of the blue and wreak havoc. So how else would you cope with such life-threatening uncertainties other than by yielding up belief in self-determination? In conversation, the phrase 'God willing' peppers every thought and plan. And it was indeed in such a place that Isabelle met her sudden death, at the age of twenty-seven. Looking twice that, ravaged by disease and the accumulated rigours of her lifestyle, she had checked herself out of hospital and into a small mud house she had rented on the edge of the village of Ain Sefra in southern Algeria. Within hours, and without warning, a flash flood ripped right through the place and took her life with it. It's a feature of the territory – somewhere there is rain; a huge wall of water roars down the dry river bed, pushing every form of life before it so that liquid becomes a moving mass. Destruction is rapid, and buildings made of earth and water are reduced by water back to earth again. The very architecture seems to court its own annihilation – an appropriate end, perhaps, for a woman who did the same? Not long before, she had written:

> I've often found the longing for death so intense in me that I've sometimes almost solicited it, trying to find in non-being the supreme sensual delight. It seems to me … that I am skirting the inviting abyss of the void. Who knows, perhaps I shall let myself slip into it one day in the near future, voluptuously and without the slightest worry or concern. With time, I have learned not to look for anything in life, except for the near ecstasy offered by oblivion, and I have tasted ecstasy in all its forms … none of these forms has fooled me, and I have rejected them all … and so, without illusions and without hope, I shall carry on until the day I disappear into the shadows I came out of one day, an ephemeral and vain creature.

In this small, scorched desert village I realized we had reached the location that embodied both her projected hopes for happiness in life, and the circumstances which brought that life to its dramatic end. Here I was as near, perhaps, to the essence of her as I could get. One last destination remained – the sand dunes of Merzouga.

To reach them took an eight-hour drive across the margins of the Sahara, to the south-eastern valley of the Tafilalt, and then south, leaving the last of the oasis villages behind and entering seeming nothingness. The Merzouga dunes are the highest in the Moroccan Sahara, rising, as you approach them from a distance, like a luminous pink mirage above the unbroken bleached horizon all around. Climbing up at first light into their hills and hollows, I stood surrounded by 360 degrees of limitless, level desert floor. We were, it seemed, at last in the heartland of the terrain that drew her. Here, the mythic realm of the imagination is realized in the geography of sky and boundless distance; here, the curved horizon reminds you of the shape of the planet you live on. It seems a territory beyond political boundaries and borders, belonging to no country or nation. For Isabelle, for whom notions of home and nationality had little meaning, it was a universal landscape, belonging only to those who have the courage and the will to survive here. And for one who was always in quest of the unreachable it seems unknowable, obliterating memory and identity and even purpose – lying down here for a minute on my back, I felt dangerously that I might never think of a reason to get up again. The idea of oblivion, the central driving force of her existence, lay seductively within easy reach. I could see how, having fallen victim, as she did, to the spell of this vast and luminous space, nowhere else on earth would be powerful enough, because it is absolute.

Its stillness is deceptive – though static from a distance, the sand is always moving in tiny fluid trickles, closing over the tracks of those who have passed. The silence is loud – more than the absence of noise, an active power that absorbs and disperses any sound that intrudes upon it. It seems like a land at the beginning of time, some harsh Eden where there is only one of everything – one shrub, one clump of grass, one distant human being, one beetle scurrying across its surfaces. Only here, perhaps, could Isabelle create herself from scratch as she had dreamed, and start anew:

If a voice shouts at me … 'Foreigner! European!', I'll not turn around. If the voice says, 'You, woman! Yes, woman!', I'll not turn around. No, I'll not even turn my head, even when it whispers 'Isabelle Eberhardt', even then I won't turn around. But if it hails, 'You, you there, who need vast spaces and ask for nothing but to move. You alone free, seeking peace and a home in the desert, who wish only to obey the strange ciphers of your fate' … Yes, then I will turn around, then I'll answer: 'I am here, Si Mahmoud.'

Sand dunes of the Sahara.

MEXICO
Damian Gorman

We were coasting along at 38 000 feet. I was heading to Mexico for the guts of a month. I was on my way back to my seat just in time for the film, when it hit me out of the blue – like turbulence: 'Shit,' I thought, 'I'm at 38 000 feet. I'm heading to Mexico for the guts of a month!' I was amazed at this, though it wasn't exactly news. And I couldn't settle to the film, I was so excited.

And yet I had never dreamed about Mexico. I was going because I was asked, and because I was interested – interested in stepping outside of the life that I knew; interested in Cortes, whose journey of conquest would give me my journey through the heart of Mexico; interested in looking around me, and meeting people along the way.

But I was nervous, on several counts. First of all, my store of Spanish was poor. I am a writer, language is my currency, but here I was going into a situation where I had no coin. I was curious to see if I would be able to find ways across the high, wide barrier of language, to be beside people. I was also anxious for the filming to intrude as little as possible into the film, if that doesn't sound stupid. What I mean is that I wanted my encounters with people – both on and off camera – to be as genuine as possible. And I had a general concern, small but fit and active, that maybe I just wasn't up to this – that I couldn't carry off the presentation of a bright and moving film about an unfamiliar country.

Bullfighting is one of the major sporting pastimes of
Mexico. It is embraced with passion by both participants
and spectators.

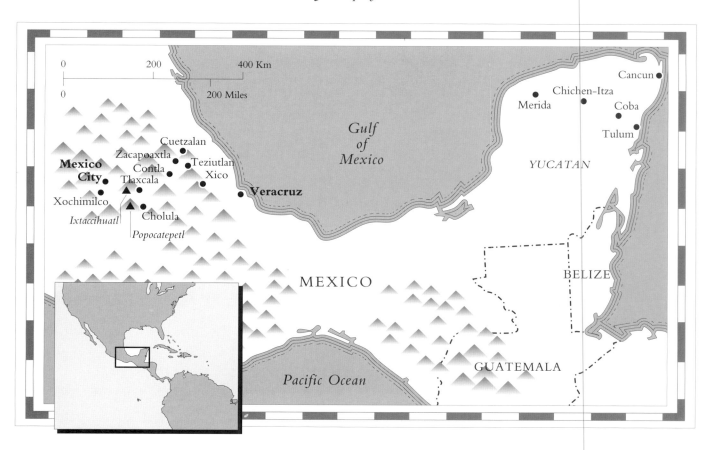

But I gave myself a talking to. 'For Christ's sake, Damian,' I said, 'wise up. What are you worrying about? Think of it this way: you have the enormous privilege of being paid to have a great adventure. Bring back impressions, warm lit-up stories, like gifts to give to your children and your friends. Do this, my son, and dry your bloody eyes.'

So on my way to Mexico, with that ringing in my ears, I resolved to be as open to the country as I could be.

Like Cortes, I touched in first on the Yucatan – which is desperately flat, and covered with scrubland jungle. He arrived in the spring of 1519 to pick up two Spaniards who had been shipwrecked eight years previously. One of these, Geronimo Guerrero, would not come. Having been spared from human sacrifice for being too scrawny, he had taken a local wife and had 'gone native'. His first child was born in Tulum, the first Mexican. Tulum would be my starting point too, and I had a contact. Back home in Ireland, when I'd mentioned this Mexican journey, my best friend's wife had said, 'If you go to Tulum I know a man there, a lovely man, you must meet him. He's American, and he wears a ponytail. His name is John.' His name wasn't John, but thanks to the persistence of a dogged miracle worker I did meet up with William Purefoy. And he is a lovely, ponytailed American.

William had dreamed about Mexico all his life. As a small boy in a small North American town he'd dreamed about making his life with the indigenous people of the

Yucatan, and learning as much as he could about the magnificent Mayan ruins in their midst. When he left the US army, after Vietnam, he came down to Mexico, and 'it felt like coming home'. For twenty-five years his dream has been sustained, and he took me through the filtered sunlight of the Coba jungle to his favourite archaeological site. As I swatted branches out of my way and tried not to trip over vicious gangs of roots, he tortured me with good-natured banter about snakes in the area. One of the most venomous, the 'four-nosed snake' – so called because its eyes look like nostrils – could more or less kill on sight, according to William. And it comes at you, without warning, from the jungle floor.

Hurdling, now, through the undergrowth I came to the 'Iglesia', a steep pyramid at the base of which some people still worship the old gods. The last twenty or thirty feet of the climb were tricky, the steps having all been worn or weathered away, but when we reached the top we were sandwiched between two wonders: in front of us the endless broccoli of the jungle, the tops of other pyramids sprouting here and there; behind us a huge red sun setting over a lake.

We were both miked-up for some inconsequential chat.

'Ma, I'm on top of the world,' I lobbed over to William.

'This is indeed a magnificent sunset,' he replied in all sincerity. I looked at him sideways, and the pair of us fell about laughing. Which, considering the height of our perch, was not a bit wise.

The next morning I snorkelled for the first time in my life, around the coral reef off Akumal. I cut lumps out of one shin, but it was a joy to swim among the blue fish, the black fish and the silver-and-white fish. I stored them up to bring home to my family.

I met up with William again and travelled with him to Chichen-Itza, which is one of the great sites – on a par with anything Cortes would have seen in Tenochtitlan, the old Mexico City itself. Unlike Coba, Chichen is always hiving with tourists. At least part of the reason, I believe, is that a lot of blood was shed there. The central pyramid, the 'Castillo', was a site of human sacrifice. On the top of the pyramid was an altar on which living people were stretched and had the hearts cut from them; then their bodies were thrown down one of the steep sides – sometimes to be ritually eaten with tomatoes and chillis.

It is not surprising that we should be drawn to blood-soaked ground; it would be odd if such ground did not hold interest for us. But I found myself being hard on all the parties of tourists swarming across the site, consuming the place. 'We are the quiet people,' I wrote in my book. 'We are here like a plague of ladybirds, nibbling on blood-spattered leaves.'

Unwilling, perhaps, to be downwind of so much piety, William asked me to join him on a small grassy mound facing one of the four big stairways of the 'Castillo'. He told me if you stood on the middle of the mound, faced the pyramid and clapped your hands, you would make a plaintive bird-cry. And he was right. It was an eerie, distinctive, compelling sound that came back.

Overleaf: The beautiful Mayan ruins at Tulum.

It was from the top of this same pyramid that a famous archaeologist fell to his death in the 1970s, having beaten the stone drums of the fierce rain god Chac or Tlaloc, and been instantly cremated by lightning. I am drawn to such stories, and as I whipped up a flock of bird-cries with my clapping I chatted light-heartedly to Chac inside my head.

But when I'd hugged William goodbye and was leaving Chichen by car, the heavens exploded and I was truly scared. The sky grew so black and the lightning was so white that it was like travelling through newsreel of a First World War offensive. There was sheet light-ning and fork lightning, fusing the night continuously. And I was in a large piece of metal. And metal conducts.

It's funny how all your sophistication can fall off at moments like that. Perhaps I had been a mite too flip with Chac? It's strange how the old, old thoughts and fears stick around.

I left the Yucatan for Veracruz and arrived on Good Friday, just as Cortes did. In my early thirties, just as Cortes was. And there the similarities end. Or almost do. Cortes was a soldier and adventurer. I am not. He was a 'man's man', which I've never wanted to be. But he was also a warmish, manipulative bastard (guilty). He was a person driven by dreams. And so am I.

San Juan de Ulua, which lies just off Veracruz, was the first real toe-hold the Spanish had in Mexico, and the last place they relinquished three hundred years after arriving. Now it has a reputation as the country's party town. People who can't do their own thing in their own place come and do it in Veracruz, or so it is said. 'We have the courage to be happy here,' I was told, in suspiciously aphoristic English.

Not being noted for 'getting up and getting on down', I wasn't quite sure how I'd plug in to party town. But I needn't have worried. On Good Friday night I was sitting at a table on the main square or *zocalo,* being serenaded by a band of mariachi musicians, when a smiling man dangled in front of me a set of electrodes the size of skipping rope handles. I (as you would) took a friendly hold of them. The Smiling One worked at a dial around his waist, and the next thing I knew my arms had shot bolt upright, and were straining to leave their sockets altogether. My Spanish wasn't up to this so I tried a few basic, very basic, words of English. But the voltage was upped and I roared off again with both arms stuck in the air, like a nutter who'd just been elected 'Nut of the Year'. I was charged five pesos – about £1 – for the privilege. And sure it lifted me out of myself, if nothing else.

I came back to earth on Easter Saturday, with a visit to Cortes' house outside Veracruz. The extraordinary thing about this place is the way that the roots have taken it over. I know it's just an accident of botany, but it's hard not to link in the unchecked growth with the tendrils of a very powerful ambition once housed there. It seems such a suitable dwelling place for a person of fierce desires and fierce achievements.

'So why don't I warm to the man?' I asked myself. Was it because his achievements were so fierce? Was it an Irish anti-colonial thing? As I headed back into town I counselled myself not to take it so personally. But I resolved as well to use this special time to examine my own drives, to listen in to my engines.

I was ready to leave Veracruz and begin my journey inland to Mexico City. I had just joined the crew in the *zocalo* for some late-night refreshment when this woman walked up to our table out of nowhere. 'Why are you wearing the same shirt for three days now?' she asked me very evenly, and I was flattered – flattered that someone should notice this thing about me. I explained it was to do with continuity and so on. She said that she'd like to talk to me, and asked if I'd go for a walk with her somewhere. In my pale heart a committee of old men deliberated. *'Talk?* What does she mean by talk? And as for a *walk* …'

But I knew that if I was to be frightened of walking and talking, I might as well give up on this and every other journey. So I went with the woman – I walked with her to the sea-front. And she gave me a beautiful present – a piece of her story. She told me about her life in Veracruz, her hopes for her two young children and herself. She told me about the dreams she has of her dead child – dreams in which the youngster takes her by the hand across a lovely quiet sandy place, where only the child leaves footprints for that is his world. She told me about the new life she hopes for in Canada, and how she occasionally leaves the kids with her mother and walks around Veracruz looking for someone to talk to.

There was much, much more, but I cannot reproduce the humour and the frankness of her talk. Underneath the sky in Veracruz – in an open-handed, undemanding way – a person gave me a little piece of her heart. And that isn't something that happens every day. Her name was Martha, and in opening up to me she made me feel welcome, even special, in her country. I felt myself starting to fall in love with it then. And I'd nearly missed out on that by being stupid, being awkward and reticent to the point of crudeness. I was so relieved that I'd found a spoonful of courage – the courage to walk and talk in Veracruz.

I told Martha that next day I'd make a wish for her, that things would turn out well. And so I did. I had time to, because my little train into the mountains was delayed by a regiment coming home from Chiapas, where a peasant rebellion had just about been defused. Mexico was tense in places. I was not. I carried myself with singing on to the train, and swanned about in uncharacteristic fashion. A very old woman said I had nice blue eyes, and if she were a few years younger … I could have kissed her (if I'd been a few years older), which goes to show how little it takes to feed you when you're full.

The train climbed into the hills like a boat through light, throwing up splashes of colour around the windows. My cup was running over, and when I left the train the guard very shyly gave me a miraculous medal, to protect me on my journey. I was touched.

How many good things can a day contain and be real? But mine wasn't over yet. I was to meet Tia Nina, and come face-to-face with the special dish of her house, *pollo mole poblano,* chicken and chocolate. Tia Nina is in her seventies, though you wouldn't believe it. She runs her restaurant with great charisma and style. I could see her presenting her own series on Channel Four – *Tia Nina Entertains* or *Buen Provecho.* She bustled around the kitchen as she made my *mole,* working the camera, letting me taste this and that. And,

having been congratulated on her professionalism, she said she thought we were 'quite' professional too.

She is funny and warm, and has no airs or graces at all. Her dessert menu features, for example, 'the pudding of three milks'. A creation, I wondered, of mares' milk and sheep's milk and goats'? But no, it's a blend of Carnation and cows' milk and Nestle's. Which wins marks for presentation, if not for content.

The taste of the *mole* was rich and complicated. Which was handy for me, since Tia Nina didn't speak any English, and I was able to manage *'rica'* and *'complicado'*. I couldn't finish it all, which caused a flutter of concern. Tia Nina said she thought I was *'triste',* which threw me a little. I was only sad at leaving a day like that behind.

From her village, Xico, I left the beaten track. The route from Veracruz to Mexico City was nearly as straightforward in Cortes' day as our own. But the emissaries of the Aztec emperor Montezuma deliberately led the Spanish all round the houses, which is why I was up in the mountains on their tracks. I rode all day from Xico to Xico Viejo, an Aztec fort in the time of the conquest, and now a tiny village with no plumbing, electricity or streets.

But I need to go back on the phrase 'I rode all day'. Before I arrived in Mexico I had spent exactly three hours on a horse – a docile creature called Sid, from a pony trekking centre. Sid was a dear, but he loved to stop and eat daisies from the roadside. It was like riding along on a high, herbivorous mattress. Cucaracha, my Mexican mount, was a different matter. She liked you to know what you were doing, which was unfortunate. And she was ridden, like most Mexican horses, with only one rein. I was learning very quickly that I'd have to do things on this trip that I'd never get round to in a million years at home – like riding a horse at full pelt, or talking to people.

I talked the hind leg off my muleteer Miguel, venturing well beyond the borders of my simple Spanish into the badlands of unrestricted chat. And inevitably I got lost, but Miguel was the soul of discretion itself. There was the time we were nattering about our domestic circumstances, and I told him I had a girlfriend of twelve years' standing. Or at least that is what I'd intended to tell him. But sadly *'tengo una novia de doce años'* means 'I have a twelve-year-old girlfriend', which I then compounded by telling him that we had two children – one seven years old, the other twenty months. But Miguel only nodded. *'Que bueno, que bueno,'* he said. 'That's nice for you.'

By the time we reached the village I was tired, but I was also a man transformed. It had given me pleasure to be able to grow in confidence on the horse. I'd enjoyed the physicality of the day, and I felt a distant stirring of testosterone. I pushed the hat back on my head, unbuttoned my shirt, and spat on the dry ground with great deliberation. I was just about to slough my arm across my chin, like a great plane shaving the toughest wood on the planet, when I suddenly felt ridiculous, and dismounted. In any case I hadn't wanted to arrive in

Climbing by train into the hills beyond Veracruz.

Villagers in Xico, home of Tia Nina and her pollo mole poblano.

*Damian, accompanied by his guide, sets out on horseback
from Xico towards Xico Viejo.*

*Opposite: Mexico is a land of horses, originally introduced
by the Spaniards.*

Xico Viejo on my high horse. I'd have felt a bit like Cortes arriving that way. So I left my horse with Miguel, and I stared at the villagers staring at me. I looked for a way in. I felt like a fish in a field.

One of the pleasures of filming this journey for me was to meet up again with my friend Hugh Thomson, the director. And to work with him again, because he films in a way which doesn't look on people as eggs to be used in his omelette. He is careful and considerate but, even so, I thought we'd have our work cut out in Xico Viejo. How were we to be present in that place, a place where many people hadn't heard of the English language? There's an idea that simply by looking at something you change the nature of it. Well, how were we *not* to change that place for the worse, by looking at it through a television camera?

Hugh and I decided we should stay there for a few days. But, though we were welcomed, the first night was uncomfortable for me. I didn't hit it off with one of the village elders. '*No hay mas que trabajar,*' he told us. 'There is nothing, only work,' and I disagreed. His remark was an article of faith, not a rueful comment. And I tried to turn it into '*There is nothing but work* – discuss'. But he wasn't on for discussion, and that was that. I had wanted to talk about dreams and realities with the villagers – the heart of their lives, their yearnings and their loves. In this I was too unsubtle and impatient. But Hugh knew what he was doing, when he broke the news that at home he had a cat called James. They warmed to him, though by far the most engaging thing they heard from us all night was that when it was teatime in Xico Viejo it was already midnight in our countries. That had them in kinks.

I felt I was getting the measure of the meeting – keep it simple, keep it domestic, keep it short. And I told the assembly, like a man who knew his ground, that at home in Ireland an average cow could give you forty litres of milk a day. They passed the story round like potent drink. They warmed to it one by one, as I did myself – though I knew that if it was true that was accidental.

I hadn't been trying to play a trick on the people, I had simply been trying to reach them – by hook or by crook. And things became easier after that, I think. They put Hugh and me in the schoolhouse. We walked through the dark with the fireflies around us like miniature dancing stars.

I woke up in the morning missing home. Around the walls of the school there were pictures and shapes to help the children learn their letters and numbers – an 'm' in the shape of a baby lamb, for example. And they made me miss my youngsters even more.

Over the next two days I was stopped and asked if the thing about daytime and night-time was really true. People just couldn't get over the fact that it was. And again I heard them saying that 'life is work'. And again I challenged that, without success.

I met a woman who spoke the old Nahuatl, the Aztec tongue that Cortes would have heard. She was well in her eighties, and told me in gleeful cackles the words for bread and fire and houses and children. She was, as many Mexican people are, so deeply polite that

*Above and overleaf: High in the green hills lies Xico Viejo,
once an Aztec fort and now a tiny hamlet without streets or
modern services. Soon a road will arrive in this distant,
unspoilt place where some old people can still speak Nahuatl,
the ancient Aztec language that the conquistadors would
have heard.*

it breaks through into kindness. Her neighbour wanted to give me relics that he'd found from the days when there'd been a fort above the village, and could not understand why I wouldn't take them.

Xico Viejo is beautiful, and remote. It is full of turkeys and lilies running riot. But, although it is lovely to look at, the life isn't easy, and people have hopes for the road that is making its way along the mountain. I am tempted to say 'snaking' its way, but it's not up to me to pass judgement on how the village and the world should meet. I would like there to be places free of things like traffic and television, but I'm not sure I'd live in one myself forever. And anyway it's madness or fascist or both to think you can 'free' a people from what they want.

I was full up with thought by the time I left Xico Viejo. I felt like a person who'd eaten too many eggs. And I travelled to Teziutlan to sleep it off – in a hotel bed, with a TV switch by the pillow.

It would be easy to miss the Hotel Virreynal. It has a narrow entrance off the street, like a gangway. And, indeed, when you make your way in it's like boarding a ship. You step into a space with a weather of its own – a well-lit breakfast and meeting arena, full of brooding portraits and art deco flourishes. It was here I came face-to-face with the man himself – an almost life-size oil painting of Cortes. He had the look of someone who just might pull it off – this harebrained scheme to take over a mighty empire with fewer than four hundred men of his own. I was, for a time, transfixed – which wasn't strange, because in this land that is thick with statues, there are almost none which refer to the *Conquistador*. He complicates the thoughts of many people. One writer put it like this to me: 'We Mexicans are the children of a rape. Cortes in a sense was the rapist, but he is our father. We acknowledge him as the only father we have. But we do not love him, and we never will.'

I watched the TV in my room for hours, without thinking why. Every time I have entered a hotel room in my life, I have turned on the TV as if it were an answering machine: 'Any messages? Is there something I should know?' And nine times out of ten it's about as rewarding as looking through a square hole at the wall. I realized in Teziutlan that some of my strangest time on the trip was being spent on my own watching cable television. I am haunted, still, by an advert that I saw for a 'solar-powered, self-ventilating golf cap'.

It was time to do some shopping of my own, and I went to Zacapoaxtla to hitch a ride into Cuetzalan for the Thursday mini-market. Outside, the hills had brewed a mountain fog which made a ghost of every moving thing. A young man offered me a lift for a little money, and I surfaced in Cuetzalan an hour or two later.

There is maybe a way of conducting yourself at a market which allows you to do your business with grace and poise. But in no time at all I had caused a friendly ruction by buying some woven belts off two Indian women. Their colleagues completely surrounded

Pages 222 and 223: Early morning in Zacapoaxtla.

me, like skin. Wherever I went in the market, they went too. I spent every penny I had on more belts and armbands, but they continued to press me until they realized that I actually had more merchandise than them. I draped it around me to emphasize the point.

At the market I ate a dozen or so raw chillis, in support of an idle remark I had made to Hugh that I have the constitution of a rhino. It didn't start out as a boast, just a statement of fact. But as the adventure continued to whisk my hormones, I announced one day that the chilli had 'not been born' that could see me off. And I lived to regret that deeply.

Cuetzalan was the northernmost settlement I would visit on my journey, but it wasn't the most remote – nor was Xico Viejo. For Contla is a point in the true back of beyond, and that's where I headed for next, with my trusty tent. And my less-than-trusty skills at tent erection.

As I went along I thought about the Indian people – the descendants of the pre-Hispanic races. I loved to look at them, and to be beside them. I was only a visitor, parachuting in for a while, but it seemed to me that they provided disproportionately few of the 'visible' people – the news-makers, the politicians. It's imagistic and broad, but it seemed to me that too many of them moved about like hidden people, people who lived on the bottom of an ocean – silent, circumspect and under pressure. And maybe that pressure was just beginning to tell. Aside from Chiapas, in the week before I arrived there had been an assassination that shocked the country, and a major hostage-taking which held it in thrall. No one seemed totally sure what was going on. As a Northern Irish person, I sympathized.

In Contla, pitched on a spur above a canyon, in spaghetti-western Mexico at last, I had my severest attack of homesickness yet. One thing that I'd noticed continually on the journey was how often whole Mexican families roamed the streets together, visibly happy to be in each other's company. I kept seeing youngsters the same ages as my own, and I honestly wanted to borrow them for a hug – just to feel that very particular weight in my arms.

I went for an evening stroll and, on my way back, I had to veer round a scorpion, yellow like the sand, with black markings on its claws and along its spine. I had decided at the outset that, as far as possible, this journey should be genuine, for real and blahety-blah. I revised that decision, instantly, on seeing the monster, but I carried on down the hill despite myself. I went through my tent like a scorpion's nemesis, and slept very soundly – thank you very much.

In the morning I drank it all in – the canyons and peaks, like the wishings or ravings of the earth itself. On the mountaintops there were straggling lines of trees, like bands of ragged soldiers in retreat. The white sun was diffused throughout the sky, magnesium-bright, and very hard to look at. And then, from out of the ether up the valley, broadcasting to the cacti and crustaceans, came the sound of Radio Mountainside or something, blasting out country-and-western mariachi.

Damian sits by his campfire as night falls.

Overleaf: Damian in spaghetti-western country, near Contla.

It was genuinely strange, but the day was young. And I left the resounding wilderness for an appointment with a priest of Tlaloc – Tlaloc the fierce rain god, whose leg I had rashly pulled at Chichen-Itza.

I have always been interested in religious rituals. They're a way in which people can murmur about what is important, in a simultaneously public and private fashion – which is exactly what any writer ought to be doing. And they call us to the attention of each other. They remind us to be kind, in the hope that the sun will shine and the rains will come.

As a priest of Tlaloc, Don Lucio prays for rain. As a healer, or *curandero,* he treats the sick. I told him that I didn't feel exactly ill, but I was missing the youngsters and couldn't see the end of my journey.

'Are you missing your woman too?' he asked.

'Very much.'

'Then get yourself a Mexican woman.' As simple as that.

He was wreathed in smiles, which did me a power of good. And, holding my hand, he shouted, in the manner of a cranky, much beloved GP, that there was very little wrong with me.

Well in his seventies, deaf as a post, he suddenly started to sing. When he'd finished he asked me for a song, since I was a poet. And I gave him one in Irish, *'Ard A' Chumhaing','* about the tiny village where I live. I felt the song inside me as I sang. We were standing outside Don Lucio's house in the twilight, and I was singing my heart out to him, and his little grandson.

Yet I wouldn't give the man my home address, at first. Inside his room was a rough-and-ready altar full of Christian images, older ones, and herbs. The room was dark, and the artefacts unfamiliar, so I gave my address as 'c/o the BBC'. You can't be too careful, I thought. Well, yes, you can. Especially if someone's been funny and kind with you. Especially if you claim to be interested in spiritual practice. Especially if a person is meeting you more than halfway.

My initial reaction came out of a story I'd heard. In the days of Cortes, when the Aztecs of Montezuma were the major indigenous power, they exacted tributes. And one of those tributes was people for human sacrifice. But the gods were voracious, especially the god of war, and his special requirement was prisoners taken in battle. So the Aztecs devised an annual season of false wars, occasioned by nothing but the appetites of the gods. They made 'Wars of the Flowers' on their neighbours, who grimly colluded. And I was told that the 'Wars of the Flowers' continue today – in a remote part of Mexico, between consenting adults. Admittedly on a small scale, but who was counting?

And into the depths of this I'd dipped a brush, and thought of tarring old Don Lucio with it. Simply because he subscribed to some of the old ways. And I was a long way from home. And a bit of a herbert.

I sobered up from my Dennis Wheatley bender, and gave the *curandero* my address. But it made me think that when Cortes and his men were travelling where I'd just been, they must have had plenty to keep them awake at night. They'd been told that the Aztec army up ahead was a hundred thousand strong, and would have their guts for starters. The Spanish had their dreams of glory to sustain them, and their own religion. But they needed earthly allies.

Tlaxcala was a kingdom ripe for such an alliance. Chafing at tribute, sick of the 'Wars of Flowers', it threw in its lot with Cortes against its neighbour, having first sized the Spanish up in a series of skirmishes. In Tlaxcala I made an unexpected friendship with Manuel Flores, a bullfighter or torero. We met in a bar and watched *Bullfight of the Day,* with him roaring and shouting beside me at the performance like a man being operated on without anaesthetic.

I didn't like bullfighting. I couldn't see the point. But 'Manolo' explained it to me with great care and feeling – the respect that he has for the bull, and his struggles with fear; how the bull, if he's able to sense it, will feed on that fear; how the crowd is a much wilder, more unpredictable animal; and, above all, how someone can prove themselves in the ring by facing down fear, and the bull, and the audience. I still didn't like bullfighting, but could begin to see the point.

It was then that Hugh Thomson pulled his masterstroke. Knowing Manolo to be a man of honour, and knowing me to be as cussed and thran as a donkey, he suggested a little contest involving chillis – of which he had brought several dozen, just in case. He set them out on the two sides of a plate, and proposed that we eat our way through them till one of us stopped. Or 'gives in' or 'surrenders', he might just as well have said. 'You should look on this plate as a bull,' Manolo told me.

I ate one of the big green and orange chillis. So did he. I ate a couple of the pure green ones. He did the same. Then it started to get out of hand – he ate seven of the red ones, which were like little unpeeled peanuts made of Semtex. I saw his seven, and raised the stakes considerably. We went on like this till we'd cleared the plate completely. To the loud appreciation of the bar, we fell into each other's arms and declared ourselves brothers.

Sitting on the can at five o'clock the following morning, attempting to surf over waves of internal rebellion, I trusted there'd been enough light in the bar for the camera. And that history would record that I had finished first.

There's a painter in Tlaxcala who has worked on a single mural over thirty-five years, and he still hasn't finished yet. It's a vivid impression or dream that he has had of the history of his own people since the dawn of time. Its size and colours and the scope of its ambition give it life, and bring it off the wall towards you. It is like a secret landscape of its own, behind the doors of the *Palacio de Gobierno.*

The artist, Desiderio Hernandez Xochitiotzin, doesn't think of it as a vision, but a statement of facts. He has spent half his life researching Tlaxcalan history, and feels in a position to tell it the way that it was. But for me his mural is a dream on behalf of his people. A fundamentally generous piece of work.

Which, when I left him, made me think about my own work. What I do for a living is make plays and poems and films. And people who do these things are often like children, who will tug your sleeve and say, 'Look at what I have made. And love me for it.' I think that near the heart of my work is an invitation to like me, but I hope at the very heart there is something stronger – a wonder at being alive. A simple wonder, at the beauties and injustices there are.

I left in the evening by bus for the town of Cholula. Cortes had come down like a hammer on that place. In a gap in negotiations with Cholulan leaders he was told that the population was stockpiling hammocks, to capture his soldiers alive and take them to be sacrificed in Tenochtitlan. Some Spaniards were ambushed just outside the city, and there were rumours that people were gathering rocks to be thrown from the rooftops at Cortes and his army. He was livid, and called the Cholulan leaders to account. They explained that they were following orders from Montezuma, but Cortes declared that according to Spanish law they would have to be punished. One hundred of them were slain, and Cortes unleashed the Tlaxcalans on Cholula. They were only too happy to take on the Aztecs' friends. Between them the Spanish and Tlaxcalans killed six thousand people, and in what has been described as 'a monument to human thoroughness' the city was ravaged, and was to suffer again later on.

Walking round Cholula with this story in my head was like having the volume of all human concourse turned down. I didn't feel the presence of the massacre in the city, but I did feel an *absence* – a very different sensation, like the feeling of walking around an emptiness. Which even the ghosts of murdered people had fled.

I based myself in Cholula for a couple of days before the ascent to the Paso de Cortes – the route between two volcanoes which the Spanish had taken before their descent into Tenochtitlan itself. I was resting up, sending postcards and so on, when I received some bad news from home. My girlfriend had just been told she had some worrying eye complaints – 'giant papilliary conjunctivitis' and buckling of the corneas. These had been caused by wearing contact lenses too long without a break. She couldn't drive or read or work, and she had the responsibility of the youngsters. I couldn't think of how I could help, short of going home. So I contacted her from the hotel to say that I would. But she didn't want me to. She said that her eyes were improving, her form was good, and our eldest was looking after her. I wasn't sure how she would manage, but I let it go.

I was worried, but to be honest I'd have been sorry to go home at that point. Not because of anything daft like 'My Career', but because I was taking this journey very personally. I had come so far on Cortes' route of conquest that I wanted to stay on till the end to see what happened. If I'd left my own journey unfinished I might have gone home with a sense of incompleteness nagging at me. Leading, in time, to me nagging at everyone else.

I hung round the hotel playing table tennis and swimming, being served fruit juice at the poolside on request. It sounds idyllic, or restful at least, and it ought to have been. But I am not very good at being served. I feel like I'm in somebody's house, and I want to

help. I would rather be bound hand-and-foot, than waited on hand-and-foot. And for some reason the waiters in the place I was staying were in bad form. Not one or two, but the liveried lot of them. I couldn't put it down to anything in particular, but I became especially attentive to them like ... well, a waiter.

You couldn't say Cholula was beautiful, but it has striking features. The Great Pyramid of Tepanapa is perhaps the most obvious. At one time, many centuries before the Spanish, Cholula was a great ceremonial site, like the more famous Teotihuacan. As a centre for the worship of Quetzalcoatl, the god of culture and learning, it attracted pilgrims from all over Mexico. The Great Pyramid is said to have been the largest ever built, and although it had fallen into disuse when Cortes came through, the top was still used for human sacrifice. In an attempt to erase the memory of that kind of thing, a later wave of Spaniards built a church on the summit. It is hard not to read that as a crowning, a symbol of conquest – one culture, literally, getting on top of another. Now the pyramid looks like a giant shapely sod, which allows the church to dominate the town. It was very embarrassing for me, as I hauled myself up it, to be continually overtaken by people running, and mobile humanity in all its various forms – determined youths on crutches; children in prams.

The symbolism of the Spanish church atop the pyramid is clear and strong, but maybe a little too tidy. It supports the idea that the Spanish came in like a major geological shift, overlaying absolutely what existed before. That simply isn't true. From the very beginning the Spanish made marriages and alliances with native people which, however expedient, complicate the idea of a dominant force in splendid isolation. Cortes himself had Malinche, a local princess, who became his interpreter, lover and greatest help. His men *were* conquistadors, conquerors of a country, but they didn't kill off its culture – for the country's name is Mexico, not New Spain or Nueva España. And Mexico comes from *Mexica,* a name for the Aztecs.

In a church in Tonantzintla, just south of Cholula, I saw Spain and the pre-Hispanic interwoven like vines. Decorated by Indians at the bidding of Spanish friars, it is probably the most beautiful church that I'll ever see. The indigenous artists kitted it out to their own tastes, with bunches of stone chillis, flowers and succulent fruits. And, among the legions of angels, archangels and saints, they managed to place some of the previous gods of their people – including Quetzalcoatl and my old friend Tlaloc or Chac. The effect of their work is moving as well as impressive – like a good choir singing. It struck me as singing in stone. But, while we had been trying to catch some of that for the film, someone had loped off with £5000-worth of gear.

I have to say something here about the crew. It's right that I shouldn't say too much about them in this, because I am supposed to carry my story to you. But there were so many times when they carried me.

Dazzling Spanish tilework adorns a church near Cholula.

I watched them react to the loss of their equipment – with dignity, good humour and good sense. It never turned up, but they didn't go into a decline. (If I, on the other hand, had lost my favourite pen, filming would have stopped for an official period of mourning.) Because mine was a filmed journey, I had fellow travellers; because of who those people happened to be, I had friends. My story would be incomplete if I didn't record that.

The evening before I left Cholula for the Paso I watched Popocatepetl smoking in the evening sun. I felt steeped in the beauty of this towering, distant volcano. I felt sovereign at the sight of it, special and content. Except for one thing: I wished Kerry, my girlfriend, was there – so the magic would have had two witnesses, two handles, and we could have carried it into the future between us.

Undoubtedly one of the strongest desires I have is to be part of a family, folded up in one, like a small boat in the waters of a harbour. In lucid moments that feeling extends to embrace the idea of humanity as my family, and helping to shelter the whole of it my concern. And it doesn't weigh me down, it makes me want to sing. On my walk to the Paso de Cortes, out of the blue, I felt like a light-headed cheerleader for the planet, and I started a concert of personal favourite tunes – picking them out of the air, enjoying them hugely, like a rambler gorging on fruit as he walked along.

All the greats of seventies' soul were represented – Candi Staten, Aretha Franklin, The Stylistics – and I even, with the assistance of altitude near the summit, attempted the high note near the end of Neilsen's 'Without You'. In other words, I was in great form altogether. I was coming to what was literally the high point of my journey, through a land-scape that was increasingly Scandanavian – with pine forests and a thrill of frost in the air.

At the head of the Paso itself, 'X' marked the spot. On a brass relief of Cortes and his band about to descend from the place where I was standing, someone had scored out the *Conquistador's* face with black paint. And they'd put slogans over the small stone monument – *'Viva las Indigenas',* 'Spaniards go home'. Which confirmed that, as in my own place, memories are long here, and grievances smart through history like cuts.

There's a feeling that, when the Spanish came down the valley on the other side of the Paso, and finally met Montezuma on the outskirts of Tenochtitlan, this was a meeting of opposites – the free-booting Spanish and the dignified emperor who had, in the words of a Neil Young song, 'his people gathered round him like the leaves around a tree'. Again, this seems like a bite-sized version of truth. The leaders, and indeed their cultures, had much in common. For example, both the Aztecs and Spanish were then pre-eminent in their parts of the world. And in the world of each, nothing happened without there being some divine sense or pattern to it. This fact is important because it gave Cortes the belief that he conquered by right and the will of God, and it gave Montezuma untold troubled dreams.

Montezuma had once been the chief priest of the Aztecs, so he knew about what had been prophesied for the people. Including the idea that Quetzalcoatl (who, among other things, was the god of arts and wind – a sane portfolio) would return from exile in the year

I–Reed, or 1519 – the year that Cortes came. It was also believed that Quetzalcoatl had a beard, and a strong dislike of human sacrifice. Cortes had both, and Montezuma – believing he might be the god incarnate – gave himself over to worry and indecision. Cortes played the legend for all it was worth, and Montezuma (this is true) tripped regularly on magic mushrooms.

When the Spanish first entered Tenochtitlan it wasn't as victors but as unresolved problems, preying on people's minds, especially the emperor's. The foreigners thought that this city built on a lake was probably the most beautiful any of them had seen. It didn't exactly seem that way to me. I came in by Beetle taxi through the *barrio* of Santa Fe, which loomed over me like a giant cliff of poverty – shack upon shack upon shack of the poorest housing teetering around the edges of an open sewer, which was brooding away like a vile soup among the people.

'Welcome to the jungle,' the taxi driver said beside me. But, like most people here, he was fond of Mexico City too. I told him that all I had were two strong rumours about it – that it was the most polluted capital on earth, and the drivers were crazy. He didn't exactly demolish either idea. He said that he had deliberately crocked his own speedometer, because he didn't like to be chided by it so often. And as for the contamination, it was so palpable that people with contact lenses had to take them out now and then, to clean off the dirt that had stolen in behind them.

I told Jesus (the taxi driver) that I couldn't understand why people stayed. Maybe it's because I've a chronically asthmatic toddler, but it seems to me that if you've any choice at all, you shouldn't bring your youngsters up in dirty air. This is breathing we're talking about, not some tasty abstraction. But according to Jesus, people don't have any choice. Mexico is a highly centralized society. The best facilities and night life are all in the city – the capital's hot! And if you want to be near the heat, you suck in the fumes.

With a kindness only to be expected from one of that name, Jesus offered to arrange some commercial company for the evening. But instead I went for a walk around the centre. I was taken by the courage and deftness of street entertainers, who seemed to prefer to work in the teeth of the traffic. When they finished they'd move up and down the lines of drivers – like water moving among stones, it seemed to me.

But my abiding memory of my first day in Mexico City is of the afternoon sun in the sky around three o'clock. It seemed such a redolent, sprawling suffusion of colour. Such a beautiful sight till you realized the effect was created by the way the smog was dispersing the light. A wonderful sunset was being induced by dirt.

Having said that, the city has its beauties too, of course. Xochimilco is one place Cortes would recognize from the water-garden city that he entered. The people there grow flowers for a living, and they move about the area on simple, flat-bottomed boats. Highly decorated ones are hired out by the hour, and I spent an entire morning drifting about Xochimilco, just looking around me and trailing my hand in the water. I love to feel sunlit and still, as I did for hours, until a man half-crazed with drink came by my boat and cracked

the man rowing it over the head with an oar. He was roaring that this waterway belonged to him, which was questionable, but my boatman's head was indisputably his own. The drunk man drenched us twice before slinking off, full of menace like an erratic crocodile.

It was in Mexico City that I first ate a plate of worms. Deep-fried and taken with strong sauce and tortillas, they were really very pleasant, except for one thing – they were kind of articulated, joined together in sections, with connective bands of muscle which were off-putting. The worms were the idea of Laura Esquivel, a writer whose book *Like Water for Chocolate* – a love story with recipes – has been turned into a film that has been successful all over the world. Laura is warm and radiantly friendly. She believes in food as much more than fuel – as magic, a means of creating your own luck in life with particular combinations of ingredients. At the suggestion of her friend Soledad I had rose petal pie, a dessert which is lovely to look at, to smell and to eat. When I'd cleared my plate I was told it was an aphrodisiac, which is not what I needed at all at that point on the trip.

Laura and Soledad both have hearts of corn, and I've a fondness for almost everyone I met in Mexico. It's kindness you remember people for, and the crack. And everywhere I'd been in the country people had put themselves out – to accommodate not only me but what I was doing. If you asked anyone for directions (and I mean *any*one) they would invariably tell you, even if they didn't know the way. It was always *'derecho, derecho'* (straight ahead). Which, as long as you're pointing the right way, it always is.

I found myself revisiting in Mexico City a thought that I'd had before, but had been suspicious of – that the Mexicans are like the Irish: full of heart; melancholy, given to drink and bouts of fun. That's a generalization of criminal proportions, but I do think we share inclinations to warmth and to gloom. Maybe I'm only talking about men here – I don't know. As far as I could see, the women weren't so changeable.

But there are other, more reliable similarities – the predominance of Catholicism, the aftermath of colonization. And a common reputation as suitable countries for dreaming – where 'south of the border' artists and outlaws can live. This veers towards tosh, of course, when you bear in mind the numbers of Irish and Mexicans dreaming of leaving.

Having entered the Aztec capital on 8 November 1519, Cortes and his allies had soon over-stayed their welcome. There was an uneasy, almost ritualized moving around each other by the two leaders until Cortes upped the ante by placing Montezuma under house arrest. The Aztecs put up with this for six months, but when many of them were attacked and killed during a religious festival they finally staged an uprising, and in the confusion Montezuma was killed. The Spanish were routed but, having holed up in Tlaxcala for five months, they returned to lay fearsome siege to Tenochtitlan. The city held out under Montezuma's nephew Cuauhtemoc, but finally surrendered in August 1521.

Cortes' former house, outside Veracruz, now overgrown with
invading tree roots and branches.

The marketplace at Tlatelolco was the last to fall. Today it is part of the Plaza de las Tres Culturas, where an Aztec ruin, a colonial church and an ugly modern government building stand side by side. In the square is a plaque which I found particularly moving – in its simple attempt to be healing about history. The inscription reads (in Spanish):

On 13 August 1521, heroically defended by Cuauhtemoc,
Tlatelolco fell into the hands of Hernan Cortes.

It was neither a victory nor a defeat, but the painful
birth of the *mestizo* people that is Mexico today.

What I found so moving was the vulnerability of the language – a quality you don't often see in sentiments written on stone in public places. That, and the yearning for unity that was in it. I thought to myself that I'd love to see a plaque like that at home – not the usual pre-set unionist or nationalist slogans, but a piece of vision shimmering in stone.

The plaque is at the front of the colonial church. To one side of it is the square where the massacre of October 1968 took place. In Mexico City, as in other capitals, students found common cause with workers in that year. On 1 September three hundred thousand people marched to the *zocalo* to express their frustration at the government. This massive protest led to talks, but the authorities were unhappy at the visibility of such rallies – especially with the eyes of the world about to focus on Mexico for the Olympic Games. Early in October a much smaller march took place beside the colonial church in Tlatelolco and, in what can only be described as an attempt to erase it – to make it invisible – the security forces opened fire. Many, many protestors were killed – the government said thirty-two; more reliable estimates put the figure in hundreds. To this day the authorities are touchy about the massacre, and seemed very concerned that I should not film on the site. I simply had a walk around it, and watched uniformed men at some fairly desultory military-type routines. They were either raw recruits or veterans past caring, for it appeared to me that people were falling in and out of formation at will. If there can be such a thing, this was funky marching. It was a relief to see something so harmless in that place.

I had started in Tulum where Guerrero's son, the first Mexican, was born. I had come to the 'painful birthplace' of the whole nation. Before I looked back I wanted to look to the future, so I consulted Aurelia Ruiz, a fortune-teller. The whole business of fortune-telling, card-reading and so on is taken more seriously in Mexico than it would be at home. I was told that the president, for example, would go for a reading. Well, I asked Aurelia to give it to me straight and strong. Whatever it said in the cards, I wanted to know.

And they said that basically everything's rosy. I've a long life in front of me – so have my girlfriend and kids. I'm to have another child, but this one will be dark. (Now what exactly that means she didn't specify. If she meant dark-*skinned,* and my girlfriend hears about it, maybe my life won't be so long after all.) She said I would be wealthy (I took that to mean in a non-material sense), and that someone in my family would take ill soon, but recover.

She ended with two pieces of advice: that there was someone I'd loved who loved me still, but I mustn't ever leave my family to go to her; and that the miraculous medal I'd been given by the train guard – and had worn continually since because of his kindness – was giving out bad vibes, and should be boiled in salty water.

Nothing, you might say, that you couldn't have done yourself – with half a brain and a packet of doctored snap cards. But I'll give her this, she told somebody else on the team that he was mad keen to write a book. And so he is.

Like the *curandero,* she held my hand when she spoke to me. In the darkness, despite myself, it was shaking slightly. Only slightly, because she was very smiley and warm, and was the image of my mother before her final illness. I asked her how things would go for her country and mine, and the cards were fairly optimistic about both. Which, though it had been madness to ask, was still good to hear.

Aurelia signed my hat – a straw sombrero, which I was turning into a super souvenir. Among the inscriptions were the beautiful and the bizarre: a Mayan blessing wishing me 'happy trails', and a message which said, 'You're the only man I've met who knows all the words to "Chirpy Chirpy Cheep Cheep".'

At 38 000 feet I was singing again – 'South of the Border Down Mexico Way', lyrics by Jimmy Kennedy, a fellow Ulsterman. I was humming really, bluffing my dozy way around those bits that I only half-knew. I looked out the window, and I know it sounds trite, like the end of a primary school composition, but the previous few weeks seemed just like a dream I'd had. I felt like a child just beginning to wake from a dream, who would take something back from the dream-place into the day.

And I would certainly take things back with me. The most important being this: I had always been the sort of person who would keep his coat on in your house. Maybe I'd be dying to throw it off, and *really* visit, but if you asked me I'd say, 'I'd love to, but I have to go'. I'd decided to *really* visit in Mexico. But I'd found that I carried – as so many unseasoned travellers tend to do – a clutter of empty bags around with me. Mine were marked 'reticence', 'set idea', things like that. To be able to make the journey at all, I'd had to put some of them down along the way. And now I would travel lighter – I really believed I would travel lighter when I got home.

I have Mexico to thank for that, and I *am* grateful. I had never dreamed about going, but I dream I'll return. With my girlfriend and youngsters with me next time round.

INDEX